THE BEST OF
JANE
GREENOFF'S
CROSS STITCH

THE BEST OF
JANE GREENOFF'S
CROSS STITCH

D&C

David and Charles

To my husband, Bill
Always

A DAVID & CHARLES BOOK

David & Charles is a subsidiary of F+W (UK) Ltd.,
an F+W Publications Inc. company

First published in the UK in 2005

Distributed in North America
by F+W Publications, Inc.
4700 East Galbraith Road
Cincinnati, OH 45236
1-800-289-0963

A catalogue record for this book is available from the British Library.

ISBN 0 7153 1819 5

Executive commissioning editor Cheryl Brown
Desk editor Ame Verso
Executive art editor Ali Myer
Art editor Prudence Rogers
Book designer Sarah Underhill
Project editor Lin Clements

Printed in Singapore by KHL Printing Co Pte Ltd
for David & Charles
Brunel House   Newton Abbot   Devon

Visit our website at www.davidandcharles.co.uk

David & Charles books are available from all good bookshops; alternatively you can
contact our Orderline on (0)1626 334555 or write to us at FREEPOST EX2110,
David & Charles Direct, Newton Abbot TQ12 4ZZ, UK
(no stamp required UK mainland).

Contents

Introduction

I have been working with David & Charles since 1987 when my first book *Cross Stitch Castles and Cottages* was published. It is difficult to describe the feeling you have when you see your own work in print and I don't think the excitement gets any less as you become more experienced – *The Cross Stitcher's Bible* is now in ten languages and I'm currently planning my next title, my 16th book!

Over the years I have become rather critical of some of my earlier work and in particular, the way I produced the charts. Computer charting was unavailable when I started writing and charts had to be produced laboriously, either with coloured crayons or plastic sheets, so you can imagine how relieved I was to discover I-L Soft's computer charting programme, which enabled me not only to produce clear charts of existing pieces but also to design on the screen with great freedom. My own version of this programme is now available from high street

stores (see Suppliers page 111 for website).

This collection of cross stitch designs is a sort of 'greatest hits' compilation taken from some of my earlier, out-of-print books. I have

Celebration Samplers – Our Special Day, page 16

Family Samplers – Seaside Sampler, page 38

spent some time selecting which projects to include and which to leave out – quite a daunting task as I wanted to include them all! Fortunately, my readers are fairly vocal and I know which designs have been favourites in the past, so I hope I have chosen the designs that you would choose for yourself.

I have tried to create a very full and extra-value book with as many charted designs as possible, so although the instructions are complete they have been kept to a minimum. To avoid repetition in the projects I have referred to the 'Quick Start' instructions (see feature box on page 11). Fuller instructions for those with less stitching experience are covered in Materials, Techniques and Stitches on pages 8–11. Measurements throughout are in metric with imperial alternatives in brackets – work with one or the other.

All the charts in this book are computerized and supplied as coloured squares with black and white symbols so you can photocopy them for your own use. There may be some differences in the new charts compared to their colour pictures because I may have improved the design as I re-charted it. Some colour keys have been altered because the original thread manufacturer no longer exists so I have converted the colours to DMC

stranded cotton (floss). For those of you who prefer Anchor cottons see the DMC–Anchor conversion chart on page 110.

When I was first introduced to cross stitch (by my neighbour in 1983) I had no idea of the impact this fascinating hobby would have on my life and indeed that of my family. Since then, I have collected and treasured all types of embroidery although counted thread is still my great favourite. If this is your first attempt at this addictive but absorbing hobby I hope that you enjoy this book of favourites as much as I have enjoyed compiling it and that you will find my other books inspire you to try even more counted embroidery techniques.

The section overleaf describes the basic materials and equipment you will need and the simple techniques and stitches required to work the projects in this book. See page 11 for Quick Start – brief guidelines to get you started.

Charming Cottages *– Country Sampler, page 68*

Fantastic Florals *– Water Lily Cushion, page 100*

MATERIALS

FABRICS

The fabrics used for counted cross stitch are woven evenly, with the same number of threads or blocks to 2.5cm (1in) in both directions, so when a stitch is formed it appears as a square or part of a square. The thread count is the method used by manufacturers to differentiate between the varieties available. The higher the number (or count), the more threads or stitches to 2.5cm (1in) and thus the finer the fabric. The projects in this book predominantly use 14-count Aida fabrics and 28-count evenweaves.

Aida fabric is designed for counted embroidery and is woven in blocks rather than singly. It is available in 8, 11, 14, 16, 18 and 20 blocks to 2.5cm (1in) and in many colours. When stitching on Aida, one block on the fabric corresponds to one square on a chart and cross stitch is usually worked over one block (see page 10).

Evenweaves are woven singly, are available in many colours and counts and may be made of a variety of fibres, including linen, cotton, acrylic, viscose and modal. An evenweave fabric may have thick and thin fibres and even quite dramatic slubs. To even out any oddities in the weave, cross stitch is usually worked over two threads of the fabric (see page 10).

THREADS

All the projects in this book are worked in stranded cotton (floss) (although occasionally a rayon thread called Marlitt is used for extra sheen). Stranded cotton is a mercerized thread, which means it is twisted when manufactured and has a sheen. Unless stated otherwise, divide the skein and work with two strands.

Tweeding is the term used when two shades are combined in the needle to create a mottled effect (as in the church roof on page 13 and see also page 52). When tweeding, start with an away waste knot (see page 9) rather than a loop start.

EQUIPMENT

Needles Use blunt tapestry needles for counted cross stitch. The most common sizes used are 24 and 26 but the size depends on the project and personal preference. Choose a size that does not distort the fabric. Avoid leaving a needle in the fabric unless it is gold plated or it may cause marks. A beading needle (or fine 'sharp' needle), which is much thinner, will be needed to attach beads.

Scissors Use a good pair of dressmaker's shears for cutting fabric, and keep them just for fabric, as cutting paper or anything else with them will blunt them. You will also need a small, sharp pair of pointed scissors for cutting embroidery threads.

Frames and hoops These are not essential but if you do use one, choose one large enough to hold the complete design to avoid marking fabric and flattening stitches. Look in your local craft shop for a selection of hoops and frames.

TECHNIQUES

WORKING FROM CHARTS

The designs in this book are worked from charts and are counted designs. Each square, occupied and unoccupied, represents two threads of evenweave or one block of Aida. Each occupied square equals one stitch. Some charts also have the addition of three-quarter cross stitches, French knots, backstitches and beads and these are labelled on the chart or key. Try to plan your stitching direction across the chart, counting across the shortest distances of empty fabric to avoid counting mistakes. To help prevent serious errors, rule a coloured line on the chart to match the centre.

CALCULATING DESIGN SIZE

The stitch count and finished design size are given for all projects but if you wish to work on a different count fabric you will need to calculate the new design size. To do this, look at the complete chart and count the number of stitches in each direction. Divide this number by the number of stitches to 2.5cm (1in) on the fabric of your choice to show the finished design size. For example, 140 x 140 stitches divided by 14-count Aida = a design size of 10 x 10in. Remember to add about 12.5cm (5in) to the design size to allow enough fabric for mounting and framing.

STARTING WITH A KNOTLESS LOOP

A knotless loop is a neat start that can be used with an even number of strands i.e., 2, 4 or 6. To stitch with two strands, which is what you will need for most of the projects in this book, begin with one strand twice the normal length – about 80cm (30in). Double the thread and thread the needle with the two ends. Put the needle up through the fabric from the wrong side, where you intend to begin stitching, leaving the loop at the back. Form a half cross stitch (a single diagonal), then put the needle back through the fabric and through the loop. The first stitch has now been firmly anchored and you may begin stitching.

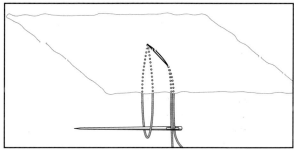

Knotless loop start

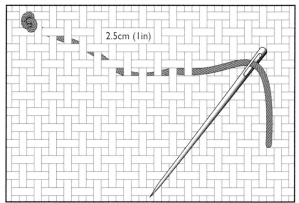

2.5cm (1in)

Away waste knot start

STARTING WITH AN AWAY WASTE KNOT

Start this way if using an odd number of strands or when tweeding (i.e., mixing thread colours in the needle – see page 8). Thread the needle with the number of strands required and knot the end. Insert the needle into the right side of the fabric about 2.5cm (1in) from where you wish to begin stitching. Cross stitch towards the knot and cut it off when the threads are anchored. Alternatively, snip off the knot, thread the needle with the short thread and work under a few stitches to anchor the thread.

FINISHING OFF

Finishing off your stitching properly creates a neat, smooth look. At the back of the work, pass the needle under several stitches of the same or similar colour and snip off the loose end close to the stitching.

STITCHES

CROSS STITCH ON AIDA

Cross stitch on Aida fabric is normally worked over *one* block. To work a complete cross stitch, follow the numbered sequence in the diagram right: bring the needle up through the fabric at the bottom left corner, cross one block of the fabric and insert the needle at the top right corner. Push the needle through and bring it up at the bottom right corner, ready to complete the stitch in the top left corner. To work the adjacent stitch, bring the needle up at the bottom right corner of the first stitch.

Cross stitching in two journeys forms neat, single vertical lines on the back, which is useful for table linen. Work the first leg of the cross stitch as above but instead of completing the stitch, work the adjacent half stitch and continue on to the end of the row. Complete all the crosses by working the other diagonals on the return journey.

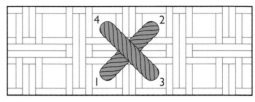

Single cross stitch on Aida

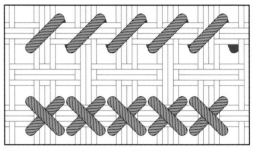

Cross stitch in two journeys on Aida

CROSS STITCH ON EVENWEAVE

Cross stitch on evenweave is usually worked over *two* threads of the fabric to even out any oddities in the weave. Bring the needle up to the left of a vertical thread to make it easier to spot counting mistakes, and work a single cross stitch as shown here, or cross stitch in rows as described above.

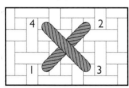

Single cross stitch on evenweave

THREE-QUARTER CROSS STITCH

This is a part or fractional stitch that produces the illusion of curves and is shown on charts as a triangle (half square). It can be formed on Aida or evenweave but is more successful on evenweave.

Follow the diagram right, working the first half of a cross stitch as usual. Work the second 'quarter' stitch over the top and down into the central hole to anchor the first half stitch. If using Aida, push the needle through the centre of a fabric block. Where two three-quarter cross stitches lie back-to-back in the space of one full cross stitch, work both of the 'quarter' stitches into the central hole.

Three-quarter cross stitch

BACKSTITCH

Backstitch is a simple stitch used for creating an outline around a design or on parts of a design to add detail or emphasis. On a chart backstitch is usually indicated by solid lines. It is added after the cross stitch has been completed to prevent the backstitch line being broken.

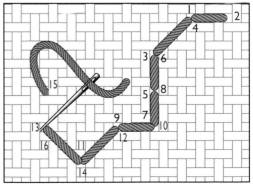

Backstitch

Follow the numbered sequence in the diagram below left, working each backstitch over one block of Aida or over two threads of evenweave, unless stated otherwise.

FRENCH KNOT

French knots are used to add detail and texture to a design. They are shown on charts as coloured circles, usually in a knot shape.

Follow the diagrams, bringing the needle through to the front of the fabric and winding the thread around the needle twice. Put the needle partly through to the back, one thread or part of a block away from the entry point to stop the stitch being pulled to the wrong side. Gently pull the wound thread so it sits snugly at the point where the needle enters the fabric. Pull the needle through to the back and you should have a perfect knot in position. For bigger knots, add more thread to the needle.

LONG STITCH

This is simply a long, straight stitch used to create flower stamens, animals' whiskers and so on. It is worked after the cross stitch is completed.

Simply bring the needle and thread up where the stitch is to start and down where the chart indicates it should finish.

ATTACHING BEADS

Some of these projects in this book include glass seed beads, which are readily available from needlecraft shops and mail-order companies. These are attached using a half cross stitch and a beading needle, as shown below.

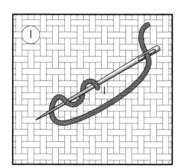

French knot

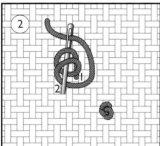

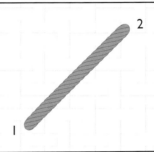

Long stitch

Attaching beads

QUICK START

All the designs in this book may be worked on Aida or evenweave, so you can choose the fabric you prefer.

- Prepare your fabric for work by steam ironing it to remove any obvious creases.

- Fold the fabric into quarters and work a line of tacking (basting) stitches to mark the folds, following a fabric thread all the way across in both directions to identify the centre point of the fabric.

- Work a narrow hem around all the edges of the fabric to prevent fraying during the time you are working.

- Start stitching from the middle of the chart and in the centre of the fabric, to avoid working off the edge of the fabric.

- Work over two threads on an evenweave fabric or over one block on Aida fabric (see page 9 for how to start and page 10 for working the various stitches).

- I work my cross stitch in two journeys, which is quicker, neater and produces single straight lines on the wrong side. I give the needle a half turn as I leave the fabric to help prevent the thread twisting. Keep the top part of cross stitches facing the same direction.

- When a group of stitches or a length of thread is completed, finish off the end carefully at the back of the work before starting a new thread or colour (see page 9.)

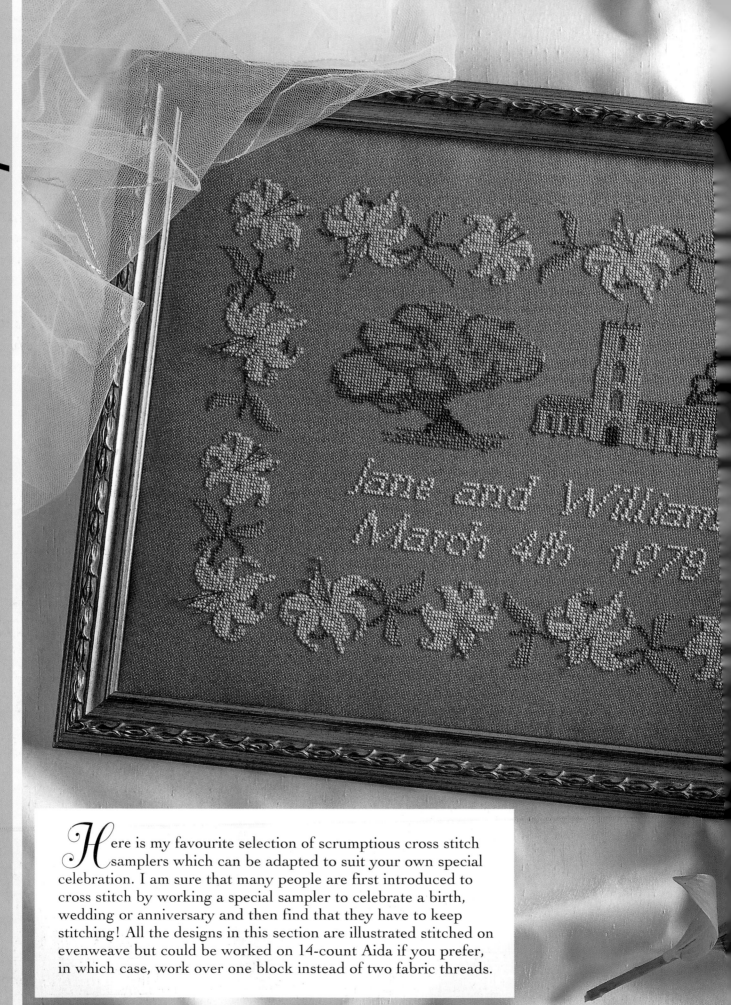

Celebration Samplers

*H*ere is my favourite selection of scrumptious cross stitch samplers which can be adapted to suit your own special celebration. I am sure that many people are first introduced to cross stitch by working a special sampler to celebrate a birth, wedding or anniversary and then find that they have to keep stitching! All the designs in this section are illustrated stitched on evenweave but could be worked on 14-count Aida if you prefer, in which case, work over one block instead of two fabric threads.

BEADED LILY WEDDING SAMPLER

This is a lovely traditional-style wedding sampler including a simple church and a lily border worked on a very distinctively coloured evenweave. This fabric could be replaced with pale blue, peach or soft green material to match the bride's accessories. The addition of small glass beads to the tips of the lily stamens makes the sampler extra special.

Stitch count: 149 x 211

Design size: 26.5 x 38cm (10½ x 15in)

Additional requirements:
Mill Hill glass seed beads, shade 00275

Refer to Quick Start page 11,
and follow the chart overleaf.

Work on 27-count lilac Jobelan over two fabric threads, using two strands of stranded cotton (floss) for whole and three-quarter cross stitches. Stitch the church roof by tweeding with two shades of grey in the needle (see page 8). After the cross stitch, use one strand to add the backstitch and then the stamens in long stitch. Add the beads to the end of each stamen with one strand of matching thread, a beading needle and a half cross stitch. Use the alphabet and numerals charted on page 106 to stitch your names and dates, planning these on graph paper first to ensure they fit the space. Once the sampler is finished, check for missed stitches and mount and frame as preferred.

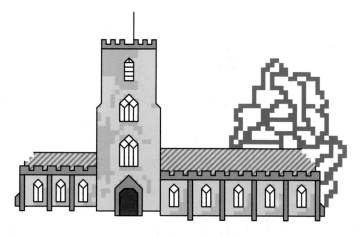

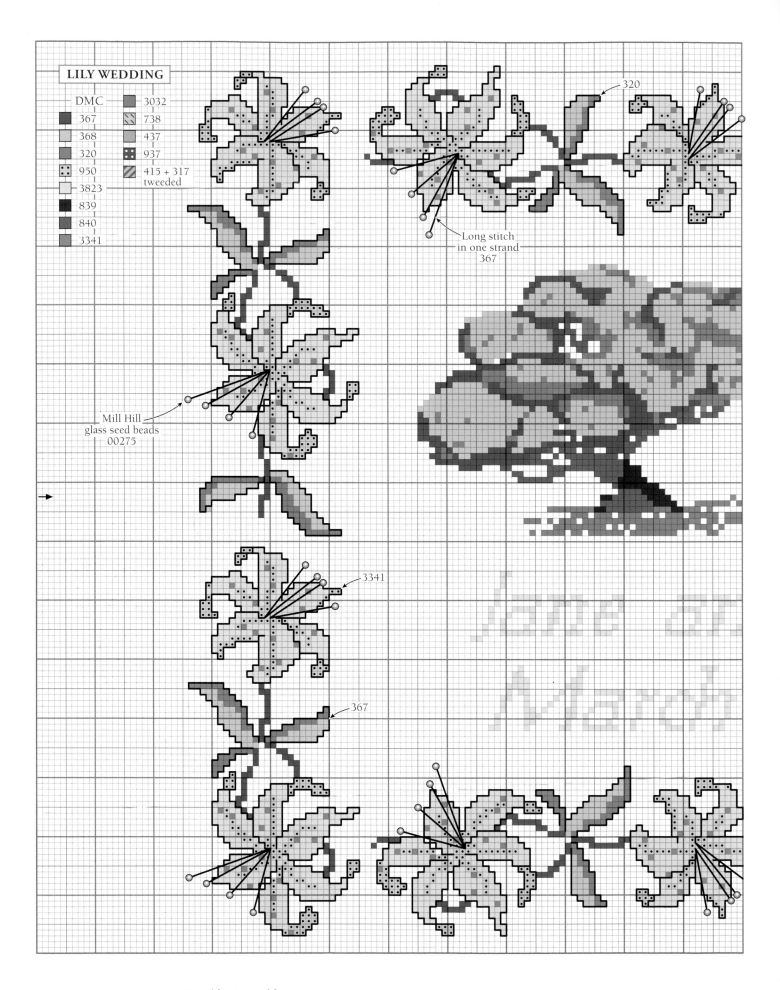

LILY WEDDING

DMC
■	367	▨	3032
▨	368	▨	738
▨	320	▨	437
⊡	950	⊞	937
▨	3823	▨	415 + 317 tweeded
■	839		
▨	840		
▨	3341		

320

Long stitch
in one strand
367

Mill Hill
glass seed beads
00275

3341

367

317

317

367

3341

OUR SPECIAL DAY

This sampler with its pretty floral border is perfect to remember a wedding or engagement.

Stitch count: 258 x 203

Design size: 47 x 37cm (18½ x 14½in)

Refer to Quick Start page 11,
and follow the chart on pages 18–21.

Work on 28-count lilac linen over two fabric threads, using two strands of stranded cotton (floss) for cross stitches. After the cross stitch, use one strand to add the backstitch and the stamens in long stitch. Using the alphabet and numbers charted on page 106, you can personalize the design adding your own dates, names or initials. Draw the letters and numbers on a sheet of graph paper, mark the centre points and place them in the correct position on the fabric. Once completed, mount and frame as preferred.

Wild Rose Card

Stitch count: 27 x 30

Design size: 5 x 5.5cm (2 x 2⅛in)

Work the motif from the chart overleaf on 14-count gold stitching paper. Use three strands of stranded cotton (floss) for cross stitch and two strands for backstitch. Mount the completed stitching into a card (see page 108).

Wild Rose Trinket Pot

Stitch count: 27 x 30

Design size: 5 x 5.5cm (2 x 2⅛in)

Work the motif from the chart overleaf on 28-count mint green linen over two fabric threads. Use two strands of stranded cotton (floss) for cross stitch and then one strand for backstitch. Mount into a 7.5cm (3in) diameter pot according to the manufacturer's instructions.

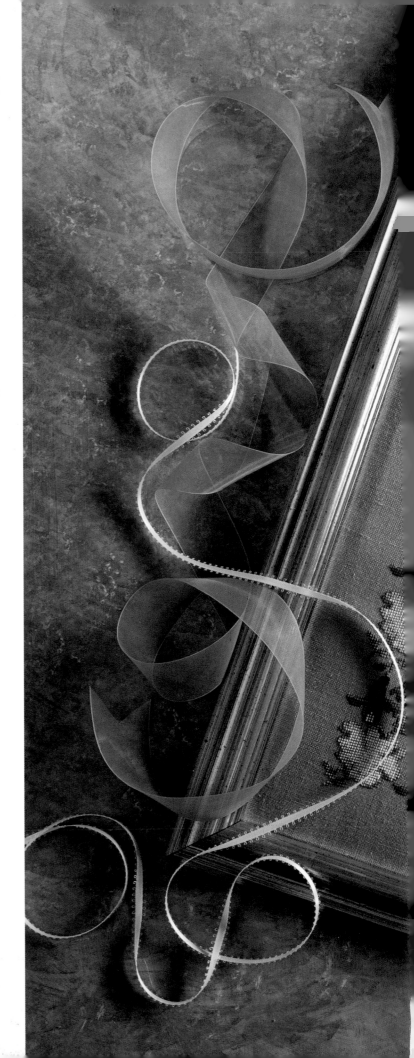

OUR SPECIAL DAY

DMC						
744	335	819	309	320	336	
369	3326	3078	3685	327	367	553

367

3685

3685

3685

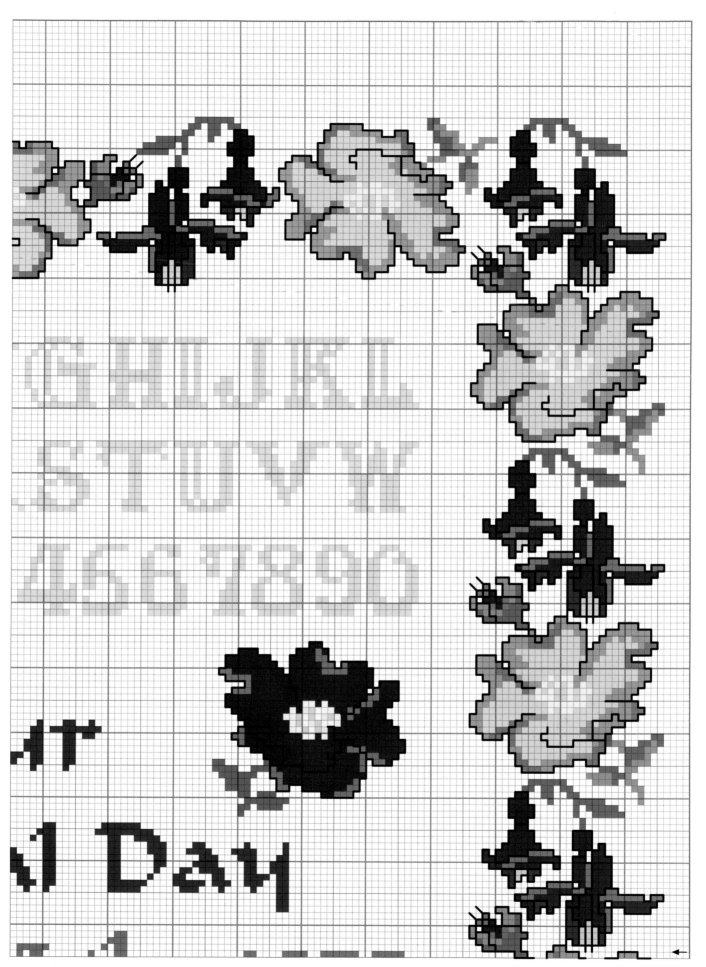

367

March

Bill

OUR SPECIAL DAY (continued)	DMC		744		335		819		309		320		336
		369		3326		3078		3685		327		367		553

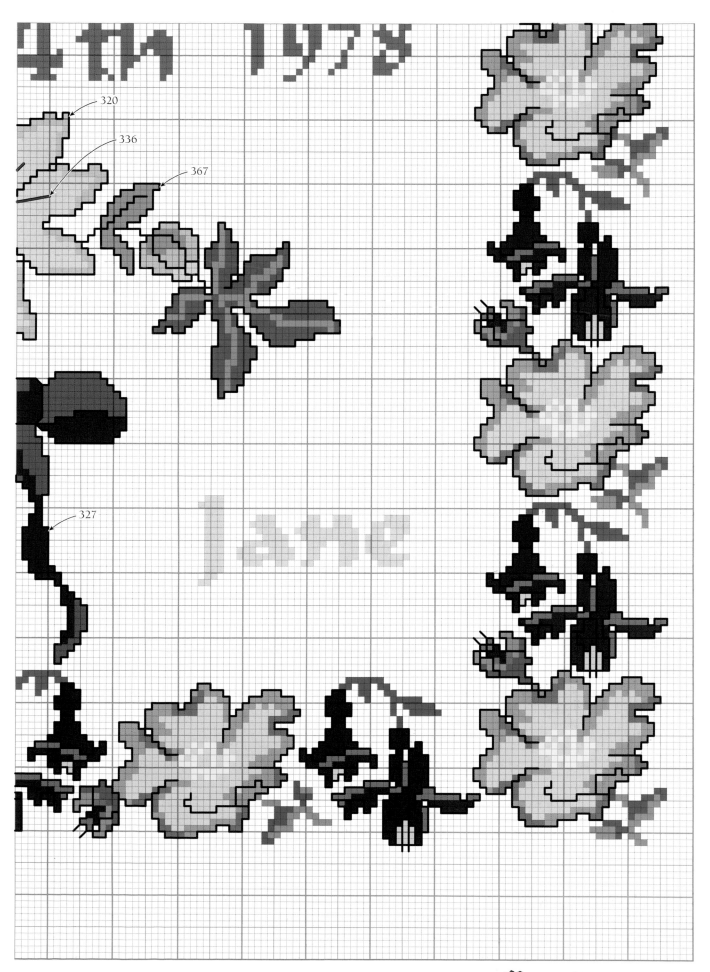

PASSION FLOWER HORSESHOE

This floral horseshoe is the perfect gift for a special bride and groom, to wish them luck in their marriage. The completed project is padded and decorated with ribbon and small seed pearls.

Stitch count: 123 x 144

Design size: 22 x 26cm (8¾ x 10¼in)

Additional requirements: 100 seed pearls approx.

Refer to Quick Start page 11, follow the chart opposite and the stitching instructions below.

Work on 28-count antique white linen over two fabric threads, using two strands of stranded cotton (floss) for cross stitches and one strand for backstitches and long stitch stamens. Press on the wrong side and make up as described overleaf.

PASSION FLOWER HORSESHOE

DMC			
▨ 744		⊠ 320	■ 336
▨ 819		⊡ 367	▨ 369

336

320

367

Making up the Horseshoe

You will need: 3mm foam core or mount board; silk dupion fabric; polyester wadding (batting); double-sided tape; glass-headed pins and matching sewing thread.

Using the half horseshoe template on page 107, trace and cut out a complete horseshoe paper pattern. Cut a horseshoe shape from foam core with a sharp craft knife. Place the paper pattern on top of your stitching and cut out the shape, checking the stitching is in the right position and adding at least 4cm (1½in) for turnings all round. Cut another shape from silk dupion for the back section of the horseshoe.

Using double-sided tape, cover the foam core with a layer of polyester wadding (batting) and trim to shape. Position the stitching on top and pin it in place around the edge using glass-headed pins, smoothing out any wrinkles (see stretching, page 108). Apply strips of double-sided tape to the back of the foam core and fold under the excess fabric, sticking in place. Remove the pins and lay the stitching face down on a clean, flat surface.

Pin the silk dupion to the back, folding under the raw edges as you go, and then slipstitch together invisibly. Using a sharp or beading needle, matching thread and a half cross stitch, add the seed pearls at regular intervals around the edge.

LACE BIRTH SAMPLER

This delicate sampler can be adapted to suit the colour scheme in a baby's nursery. Instead of stitching the baby's name and birth date you could attach a small photograph, as I have done in the variation on page 26.

Stitch count: 163 x 153

Design size: 30 x 28cm (11¾ x 11in)

Refer to Quick Start page 11, and follow the chart overleaf.

Work on 28-count beige Jobelan over two fabric threads using two strands of stranded cotton (floss) for whole and three-quarter cross stitches and then one strand to add the backstitches. You can personalize the design using the backstitch alphabet and numbers charted on page 106, adding your own dates, names or initials. Draw the letters and numbers on graph paper, mark the centre points and stitch in the correct position on the fabric. Once completed, check for missed stitches and mount and frame as preferred.

Blue Lace Birth Sampler

Stitch count: 164 x 153

Design size: 30 x 28cm (11¾ x 11in)

*This beaded variation of the lace sampler is worked over two
threads of a 25-count salmon pink linen. It uses two strands
of dark blue stranded cotton (floss) for cross stitch and one
for backstitch, though the colours of fabric and thread can
easily be changed to your preference. Refer to the chart here
for the additional backstitch detail around the beads. Add
the mid blue seed beads with one strand of matching thread,
a beading needle and a half cross stitch. The bird motif has
also been substituted for the heart motif in this version, but
you may choose to stitch it as charted. Mount and frame the
completed stitching as desired.*

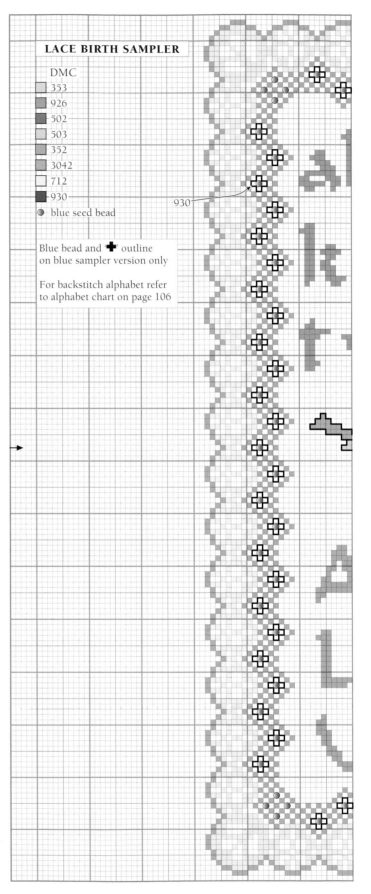

LACE BIRTH SAMPLER

DMC
- 353
- 926
- 502
- 503
- 352
- 3042
- 712
- 930
- ● blue seed bead

930

Blue bead and ✚ outline
on blue sampler version only

For backstitch alphabet refer
to alphabet chart on page 106

CELEBRATION ROSES

This distinctive rose design is illustrated in two colourways and is simple to adapt to suit an engagement, wedding or anniversary. Add embellishments to create a truly special gift.

Red rose stitch count: 99 x 146

Design size: 18 x 26.5cm (7 x 10½in)

Ivory rose stitch count: 99 x 156

Design size: 18 x 28cm (7 x 11in)

Refer to Quick Start page 11, and follow the chart overleaf.

Work the red rose on 28-count mint green Cashel linen over two fabric threads using two strands of stranded cotton (floss) for cross stitch and one for backstitch. Cross stitch the message of your choice, planning the design on graph paper first. Once completed, mount and frame as desired.

Work the ivory rose in the same way as the red but on 28-count beige Cashel linen over two fabric threads, using cream colouring (code numbers given in brackets on the chart key). Once completed, attach the charm and ribbon bow using matching thread and then mount and frame.

IT WAS A VERY GOOD YEAR

These unusual birthday cards can be adapted for any date using the numbers below each design's chart. You could also change the colour of the tulip flowers to the recipient's favourite colour.

Tulip stitch count: 65 x 122

Design size: 12 x 22cm (4½ x 8¾in)

Poppy stitch count: 83 x 144

Design size: 15 x 26cm (6 x 10¼in)

Refer to Quick Start page 11,
and follow the chart on pages 32–33.

Work on 14-count ivory Aida over one block, using two strands of stranded cotton (floss) for cross stitches and then one strand for backstitches. Mount the completed stitching into a ready-made card (see page 108). The fabric in the examples illustrated was given a light coating of spraypaint before stitching – pale green for the poppy and gold for the tulip. If using spray paints follow the manufacturer's instructions and work in a well-ventilated space.

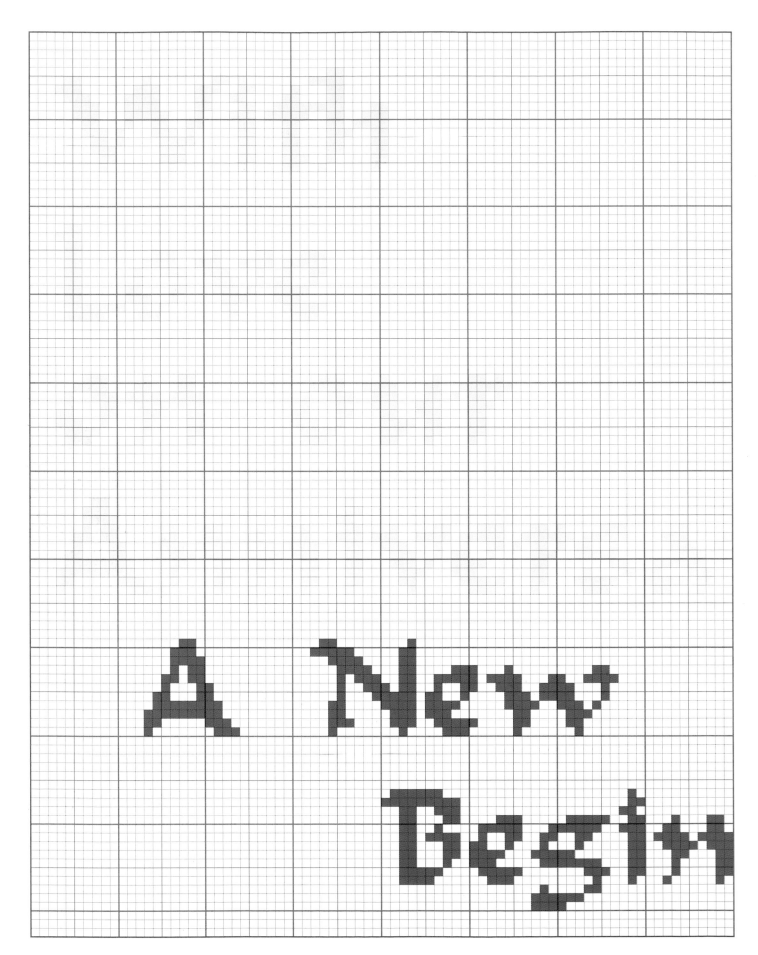

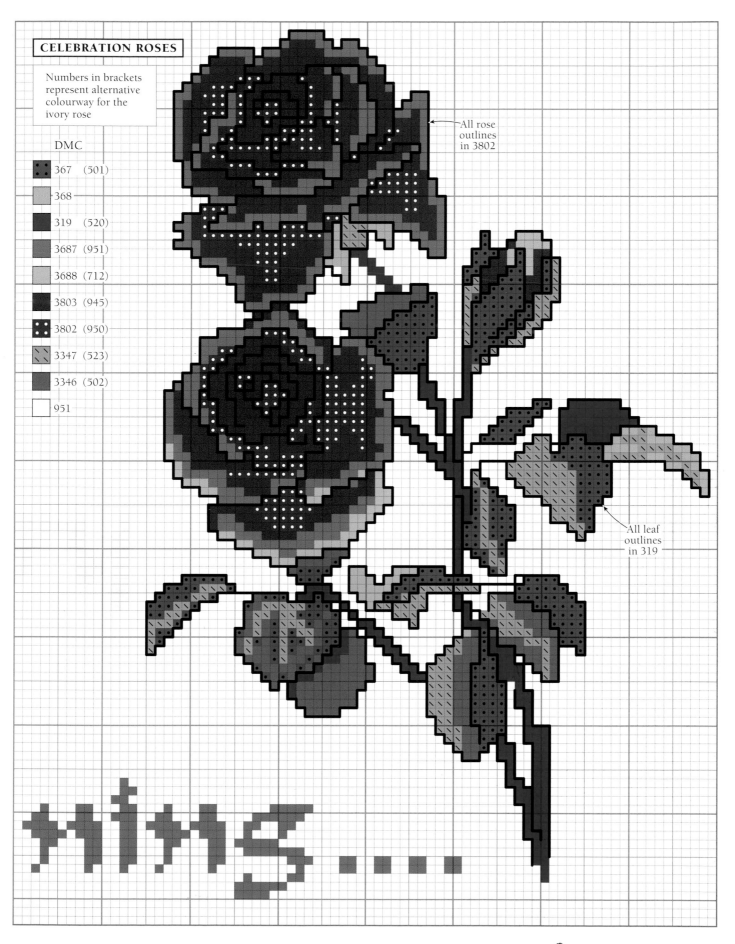

CELEBRATION ROSES

Numbers in brackets represent alternative colourway for the ivory rose

DMC

⠿	367	(501)
	368	
	319	(520)
	3687	(951)
	3688	(712)
	3803	(945)
⠿	3802	(950)
⟋⟋	3347	(523)
	3346	(502)
	951	

All rose outlines in 3802

All leaf outlines in 319

DMC					
▨ 522	▨ 3706				
▧ 520	▨ 3708				
▢ 524	▢ 3713				

ALTERNATIVE COLOURWAY

DMC	
▨ 520	▨ 676
▢ 677	▨ 725

1950 ...

was a very

good year!

0651 061895731

1950 195731 063195731

our very special mom ...

3721

520

520

520

520

This section of my book is full of simply lovely samplers including designs that could be displayed with great effect in a conservatory, den or study. Families have different hobbies and interests but many of them could be covered here. I have included music, games, gardens, animals and the seaside. I have used the seaside designs in my bathroom with collections of shells, little carved boats, driftwood and so on. All of the designs in this section could be worked on 14-count Aida fabric if preferred.

GAMES SAMPLER

This fun sampler features all the family's favourite games, from snakes and ladders and chess, to Scrabble and Monopoly. You could stitch the whole sampler to hang in the den, if you have one, or pick out key motifs for smaller projects.

Stitch count: 130 x 150

Design size: 24 x 27cm (9¼ x 10¾in)

Refer to Quick Start page 11,
and follow the chart overleaf.

Work on 27-count cream Linda evenweave over two fabric threads, using two strands of stranded cotton (floss) for whole and three-quarter cross stitches. After the cross stitch, use one strand to add the backstitches in the colours given on the chart. Work the French knots (shown by circles on the chart) with two strands, a gold-plated needle and two twists around the needle. There are a number of backstitched motifs on this sampler which need some careful counting to ensure they look neat and that there are minimal threads showing through from the back to the front of the work. Work these backstitches over two threads or one block and resist the temptation to cross to more threads to speed up the process! Once the sampler is completed, check for missed stitches and then mount and frame as preferred.

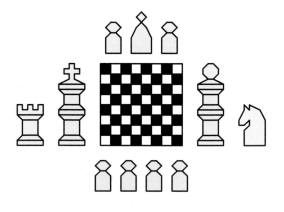

Games Box

Stitch count: 112 x 112

Design size: 20.5 x 20.5cm (8 x 8in)

This variation of the Games Sampler uses some of the motifs from the main chart. Draw the box shapes for the numerals on graph paper and then the outlines of the motifs you wish to use. Work on 14-count beige Aida over one block, following the Games Sampler stitching instructions on page 35. Once completed, mount in a wooden box (see Suppliers) according to the manufacturer's instructions and use it to store playing cards, dice, pencils and notepads and other family games equipment.

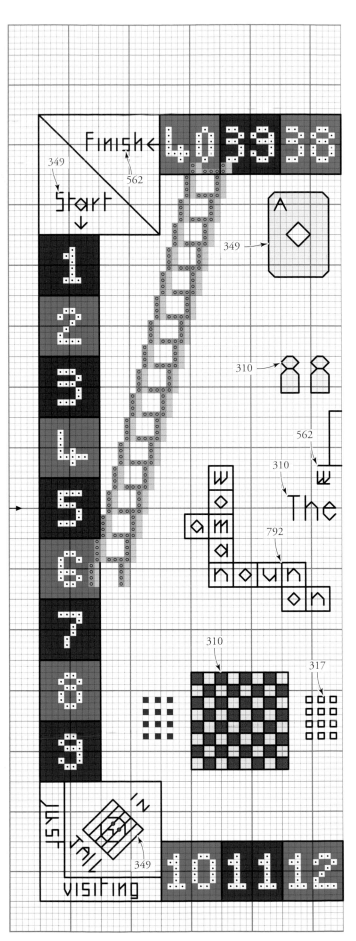

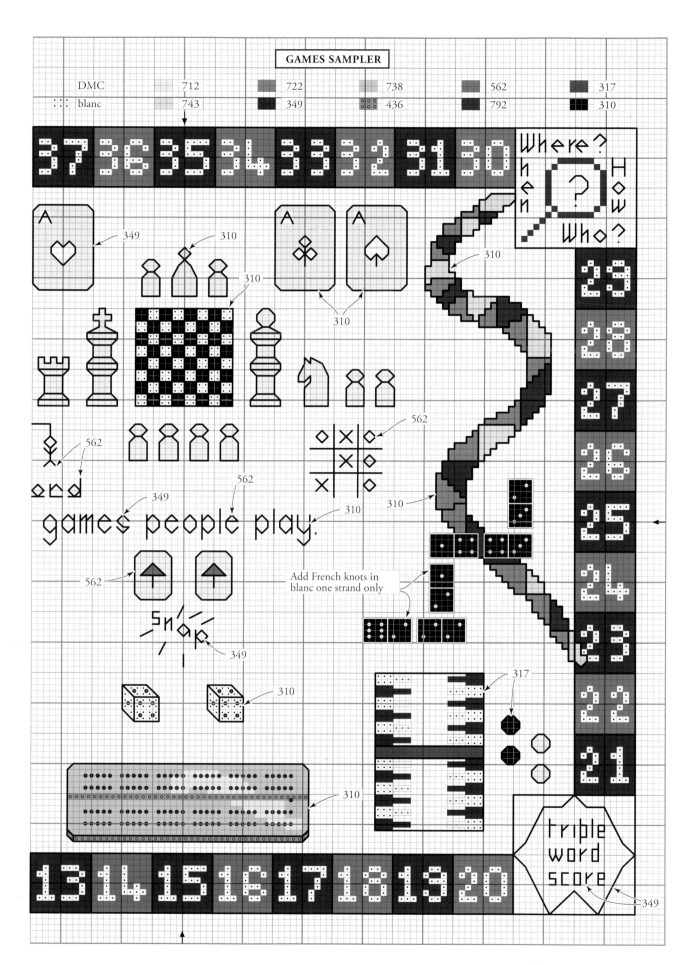

SEASIDE SAMPLER

Children just love the seaside, so what better for a family or child's bathroom than this pretty seaside sampler? They will adore the soft ocean colours and the tiny beads added to the bubbles.

Stitch count: 143 x 220

Design size: 26 x 40cm (10¼ x 15¾in)

Additional requirements:
Mill Hill seed beads in pale blue 02064 and cream 03021

Refer to Quick Start page 11, and follow the chart on pages 40–42.

Work on 28-count antique white Cashel linen over two fabric threads using two strands of stranded cotton (floss) for cross stitches. Some areas use tweeding – see page 8. Add the backstitches with one strand, in the colours given on the chart. Work the French knots with two strands, a gold-plated needle and two twists around the needle. Add the optional beads with one stand of matching thread, a beading needle and a half cross stitch. Once completed, check for missed stitches and mount and frame as preferred.

Seashell Towels

Stitch count and design size depend on motifs used

These lovely soft towels are designed especially for cross stitch (see Suppliers), but you can achieve the same effect using a linen band from needlecraft shops. Select the motifs that you like from the main chart and, after checking the stitch count, stitch using stranded cottons (floss) as listed in the chart key.

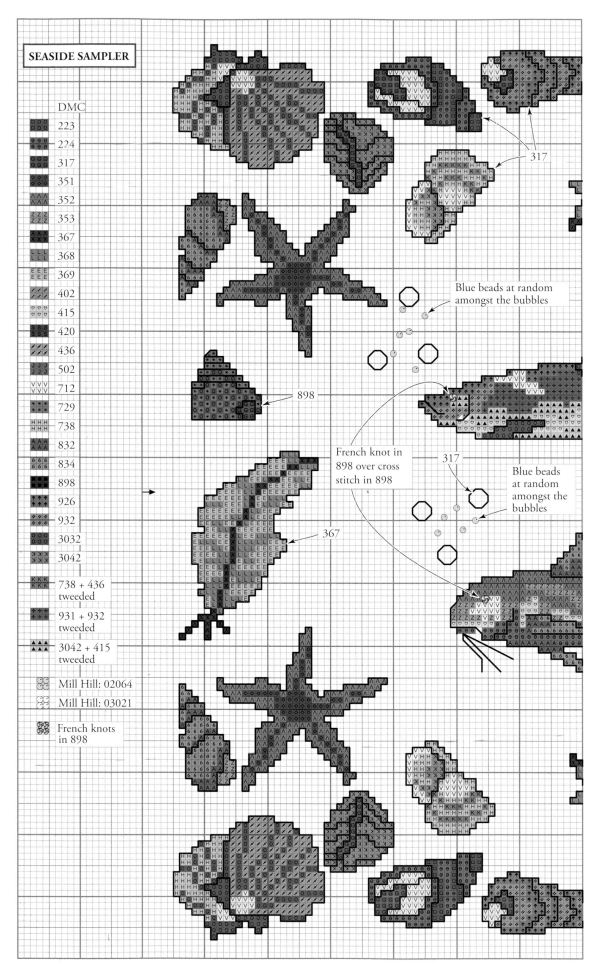

SEASIDE SAMPLER

DMC

223	
224	
317	
351	
352	
353	
367	
368	
369	
402	
415	
420	
436	
502	
712	
729	
738	
832	
834	
898	
926	
932	
3032	
3042	

738 + 436
tweeded

931 + 932
tweeded

3042 + 415
tweeded

Mill Hill: 02064

Mill Hill: 03021

French knots
in 898

317

317

Blue beads at random
amongst the bubbles

Blue beads
at random
amongst the
bubbles

898

French knot in
898 over cross
stitch in 898

367

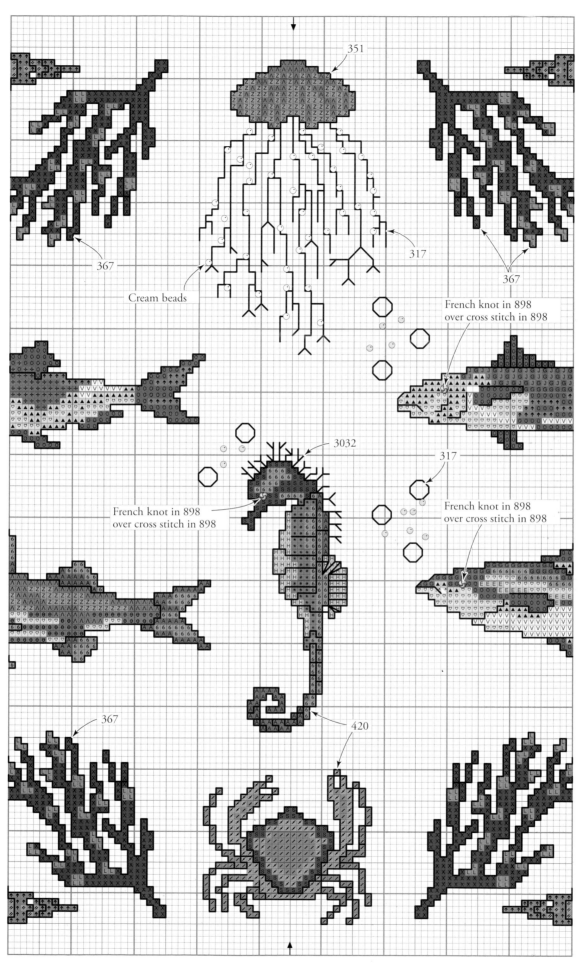

351

367

317

367

Cream beads

French knot in 898
over cross stitch in 898

3032

French knot in 898
over cross stitch in 898

317

French knot in 898
over cross stitch in 898

367

420

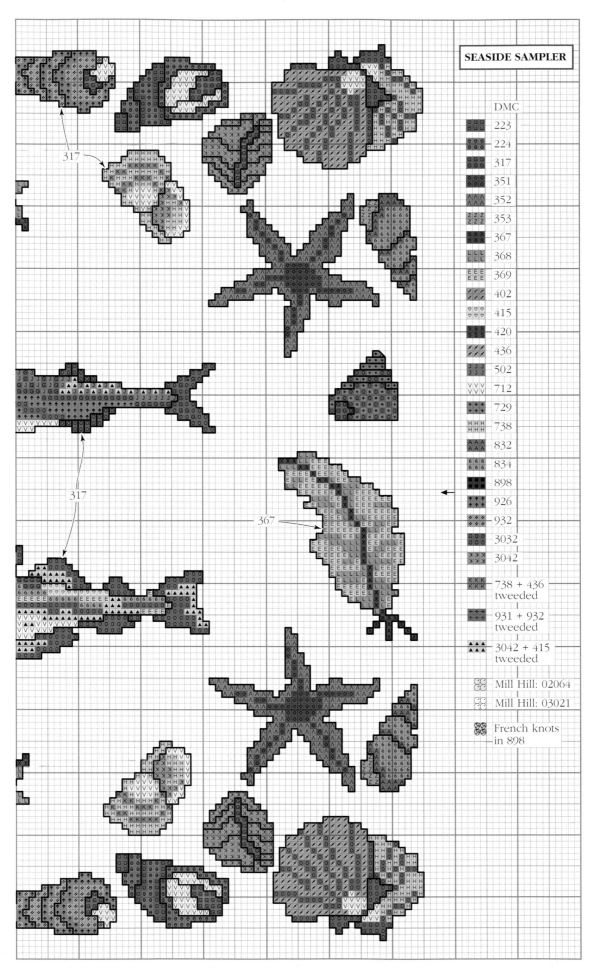

SEASIDE SAMPLER

	DMC
⊔ ⊔ ⊔	223
⊙ ⊙ ⊙	224
⊙ ⊙ ⊙	317
⬦ ⬦ ⬦	351
∧ ∧ ∧	352
Z Z Z	353
✕ ✕ ✕	367
L L L	368
E E E	369
⁄ ⁄ ⁄	402
♡ ♡ ♡	415
S S S	420
⁄ ⁄ ⁄	436
J J J	502
V V V	712
✳ ✳ ✳	729
H H H	738
A A A	832
6 6 6	834
▦	898
↑ ↑ ↑	926
⁄ ⁄ ⁄	932
O O O	3032
✕ ✕ ✕	3042
K K K	738 + 436 tweeded
✛ ✛ ✛	931 + 932 tweeded
▲ ▲ ▲	3042 + 415 tweeded
⊞	Mill Hill: 02064
⊞	Mill Hill: 03021
❁	French knots in 898

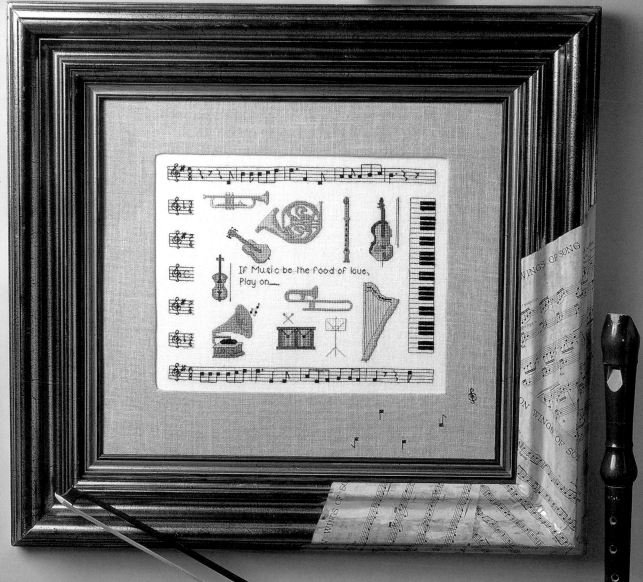

Music Sampler

Stitch count: 131 x 160

Design size: 24 x 29cm (9½ x 11½in)

Refer to Quick Start page 11, follow the chart on pages 44–45 and the stitching instructions overleaf.

When I decided to design a music sampler I was tempted to make up a musical score but then I enlisted the help of my musical husband who chose the music for me — simply perfect. This sampler celebrates all kinds of music; the score at the top and bottom is from On Wings of Song *composed by Mendelssohn, and the famous quote comes from Shakespeare's play* Twelfth Night.

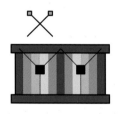

Work the music sampler on 28-count cream Cashel linen over two fabric threads using two strands of stranded cotton (floss) for whole and three-quarter cross stitches. The piano keys on the right-hand side of the sampler may be worked in backstitch only or filled in with white cross stitch. Use two strands to add the backstitch lettering and one strand for the remaining backstitches, in the colours given on the chart. This design has many backstitched motifs so plan your route carefully when stitching these to avoid too many trailing threads on the back of the work which might show through to the front. Work French knots with two strands, a gold-plated needle and two twists around the needle. Once completed, check for missed stitches and mount and frame as preferred.

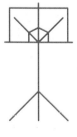

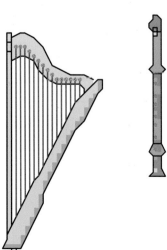

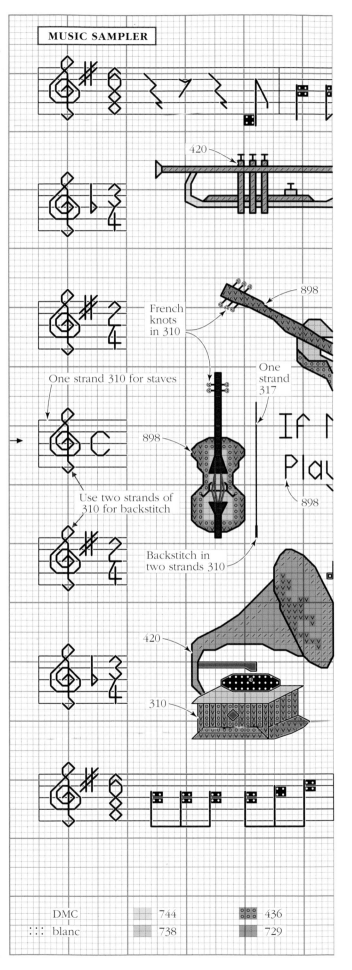

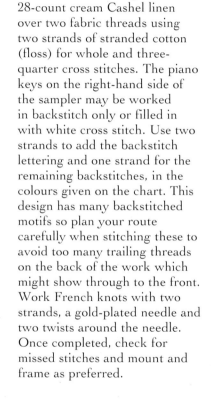

GARDEN SAMPLER

In this dreamy design, the wild rose border reminds me of Cotswold hedgerows, buzzing with bees and butterflies, and the topiary trees are reminiscent of those at Sudeley Castle in Gloucestershire, England. The motifs on this sampler are perfect for using in individual projects, as any one would look lovely as a card, box top or even a little picture. I have seen these designs worked on very fine silk gauze as miniatures and they were very effective.

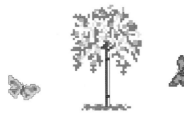

Stitch count: 201 x 286

Design size: 36.5 x 52cm (14½ x 20½in)

Refer to Quick Start page 11,
and follow the chart on pages 48–51.

Work on 28-count antique white Cashel linen over two fabric threads using two strands of stranded cotton (floss) for whole and three-quarter cross stitches. After the cross stitch has been completed use two strands to add the backstitch lettering and one strand for the remaining backstitch outlines, in the colours given on the chart. When working the poem by Dorothy Gurney in backstitch, work the stitches over two threads or one block and resist the temptation to cross to more threads to speed up the process! Work the French knots where indicated using two strands of stranded cotton (floss), a gold-plated needle and two twists around the needle. If you wish you could add French knots in DMC 350 to the flower centres around the border, and to the flowers in the flowerpot at the front of the group of pots. Once the sampler is completed, check for missed stitches and mount and frame.

The kiss of the sun for pardon,
The song of the birds for mirth,
One is nearer God's Heart in a garden,
Than anywhere else on earth
Dorothy Gurney

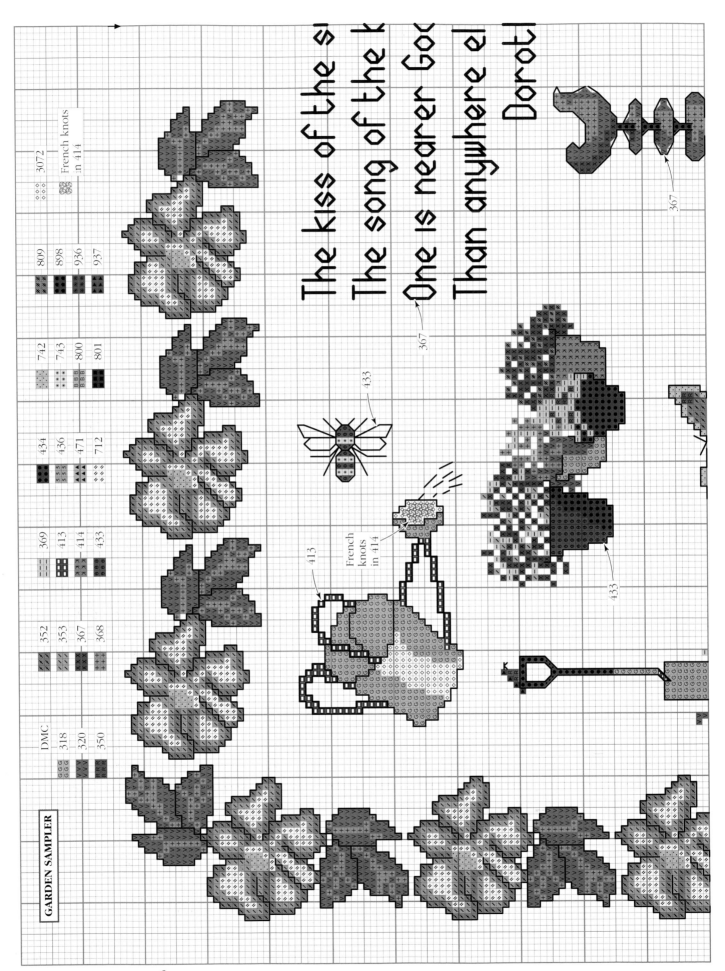

The kiss of the s[un]

The song of the [b...]

One is nearer God

Than anywhere el[se]

Dorot[hy]

French knots
in 414

French
knots
in 414

413

433

433

367

367

367

433

DMC			
318	809	742	3072
320	898	743	French knots in 414
350	936	800	
	937	801	

352	369	434
353	413	436
367	414	471
368	433	712

GARDEN SAMPLER

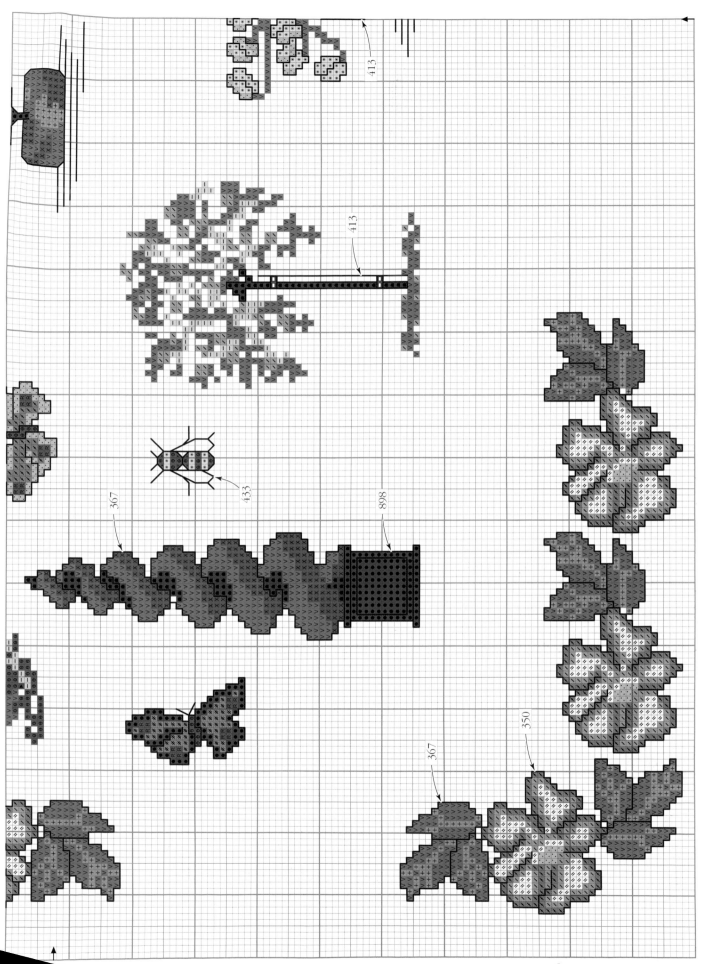

413

413

433

367

898

350

367

GARDEN SAMPLER

DMC		
318	GGG GGG	
320	VVV	
350	RRR RRR	

352		
353	///	
367		
368		

369	— —	
413		
414	✗✗	
433	❖❖❖	

434		
436	SSS SSS	
471	▲▲▲	
712	❖❖	

742		
743	✱✱	
800	BBB BBB	
801		

809	✗✗	
898		
936		
937	▲▲

3072	◇◇◇
French knots in 414	❀❀

367

413

367

801

413

367

un for pardon,

irds for mirth,

's heart in a garden

se on earth

hy Gurney

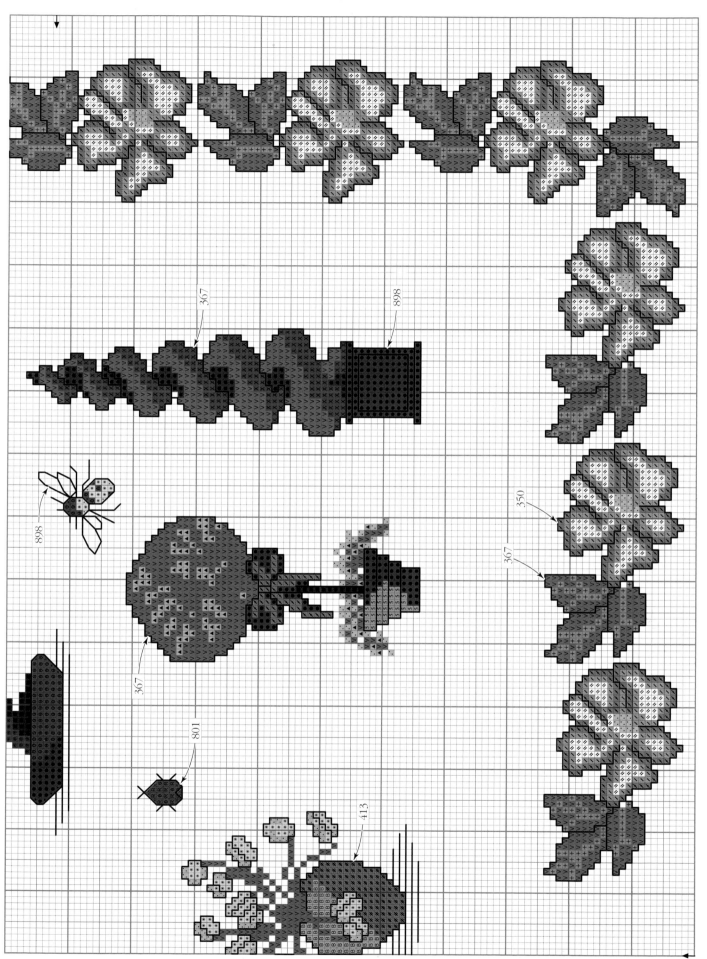

367

898

898

350

367

367

801

413

ALL THINGS WILD

This delightful sampler depicting children's favourite wild animals would make a lovely gift to a new son, daughter or even grandchild. I made this one for my children James and Louise. In the worked example illustrated, the poem is stitched in blue cross stitch but you could easily alter this to suit a colour scheme of your choice. Any of the animal motifs in the sampler could be stitched individually to make perfect little cards and gifts.

Stitch count: 157 x 285

Design size: 28.5 x 52cm (11¼ x 20¼in)

Refer to Quick Start page 11,
and follow the chart overleaf.

Work on 28-count beige Cashel linen over two fabric threads using two strands of stranded cotton (floss) for whole and three-quarter cross stitches. After all the cross stitch has been completed, use one strand to add the backstitch outlines in the colours given on the chart. To achieve some of the mottled effects in fur or feathers, some thread colours have been tweeded.

Tweeding is a simple practice which not only produces subtle results but is a way to increase the numbers of colours in your palette without buying more thread. To tweed, combine more than one coloured thread in the needle at the same time and work as one. You can also apply this technique to working French knots, to great effect. Once the sampler is complete, check for missed stitches and then mount and frame as preferred.

the love of all things wild,
the heart of the unborn child,
ve us all the will to nurture,
ve them all a certain future.

ALL THINGS WILD

DMC						
		840	367	792	435	
632		3033	413	368	801	
841		3032	310	725	838	

413

840

413

801

For the love of a

For the heart of

Give us all the wi

Give them all a c

801

801

840

SWEET PEA WELCOME

This pretty design will make your guests feel welcome, or make a charming house-warming gift.

Stitch count: 82 x 139

Design size: 15 x 25cm (5¾ x 10in)

Refer to Quick Start page 11,
and follow the chart overleaf.

Work on 28-count lilac Cashel linen over two fabric threads using two strands of stranded cotton (floss) for cross stitches and then one strand to add the backstitches in the colours given on the chart. Once completed, check for missed stitches and mount and frame as preferred.

PANSY FRAME

What better way to show people you love them than to frame their photo in your cross stitching?

Stitch count: 22 x 21

Design size: 4 x 4cm (1½ x 1½in)

Refer to Quick Start page 11, and follow the chart, right.

Work on 14-count cream stitching paper (see Suppliers) using three strands of stranded cotton (floss) for cross stitches and then add the backstitch outline using two strands. Cut the aperture for your photograph, stitching a simple flower motif and mini border if you wish, as shown in the picture opposite (bottom left).

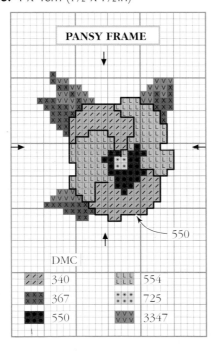

PANSY FRAME

550

DMC		
340	LLLL 554	
367	725	
550	VVV 3347	

Sweet Pea Frame

Stitch count: 72 x 72

Design size: 13 x 13cm (5 x 5in)

This photograph frame (shown below) uses the chart overleaf. Work on 14-count cream stitching paper using three strands of stranded cotton (floss) for cross stitches and two for backstitches. To form a corner border, omit the stitching that appears within the red dashed lines on the chart, then turn the section on the opposite page 90 degrees clockwise, bringing the two sections together at the star point. Once stitching is complete, cut an aperture in the stitching paper for your photograph and then frame.

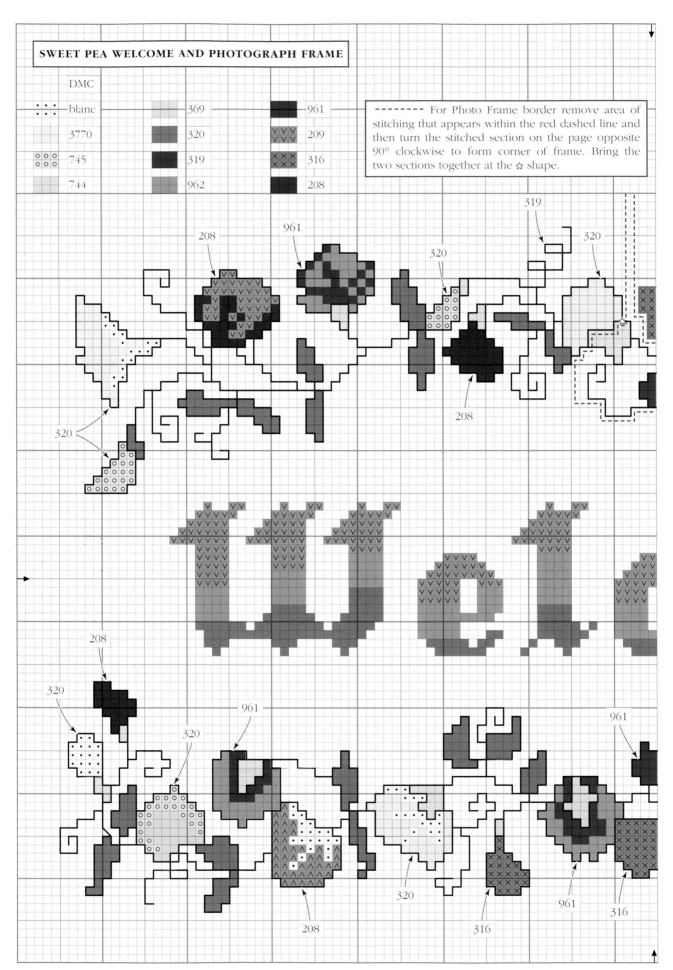

SWEET PEA WELCOME AND PHOTOGRAPH FRAME

DMC

blanc	369	961
3770	320	209
745	319	316
744	962	208

- - - - - - - For Photo Frame border remove area of stitching that appears within the red dashed line and then turn the stitched section on the page opposite 90° clockwise to form corner of frame. Bring the two sections together at the ☆ shape.

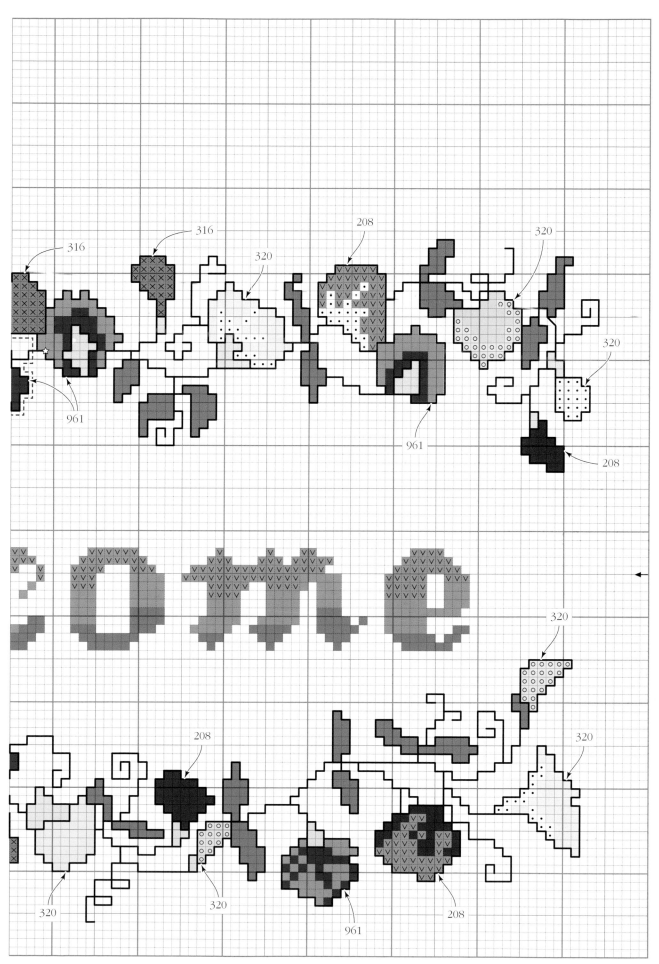

When I first started designing cross stitch charts I spent many hours drawing buildings, usually based on the lovely area of the Cotswolds where we live in Gloucestershire, England. I had great fun learning how to combine colours for brick, stone and slate. The following pages are a selection of my favourite cottages taken from some of my previous books.

THE COTTAGE COLLECTION

Make just one or the whole set of these, my best-loved cottage designs. I have included a stitch count for each cottage so you can combine the designs in different ways.

Refer to Quick Start on page 11 if necessary. Work the cottages on 28-count cream evenweave or 14-count Aida using two strands of stranded cotton (floss) for cross stitches. Some of the designs have tweeded areas where two shades of stranded cotton (floss) have been combined in the needle to great effect. Some of the cottages have simple line borders; these can be added at will and are not included in the charts provided. Add the backstitches after the cross stitch, using one strand of the colours given on the charts. Once the stitching is complete, make up as desired.

1 Moor Farm Cottage
Stitch count: 38 x 56
Design size: 7 x 10cm (2¾ x 4in)

2 Rose Cottage
Stitch count: 36 x 41
Design size: 6.5 x 7.5cm (2½ x 3in)

3 Old Barn House
Stitch count: 34 x 44
Design size: 6 x 8cm (2½ x 3in)

4 Apple Cottage
Stitch count: 46 x 43
Design size: 8.5 x 8cm (3¼ x 3in)

5 The Willows
Stitch count: 55 x 89
Design size: 10 x 16cm (4 x 6½in)

6 The Oaks
Stitch count: 47 x 69
Design size: 8.5 x 12.5cm (3¼ x 5in)

7 Crabapple Farm
Stitch count: 38 x 54
Design size: 7 x 10cm (2¾ x 3¾in)

Moor Farm Cottage — 317, 936

Rose Cottage — 317, 936

FOUR COTTAGES

DMC

◇◇◇	223	GGG	415	⁄⁄⁄	437	■■	930	VVV	3347	△▲	3830	∗∗∗	317 + 415 tweeded
⁄⁄⁄	224	●●●	434	⟋⟋⟋	738	SSS	932	LLL	3348	|||	blanc	••••	
◥◥◥	317	⁄⁄⁄	436	+++	739	■■	936	○○○	3350				414 + 318 tweeded

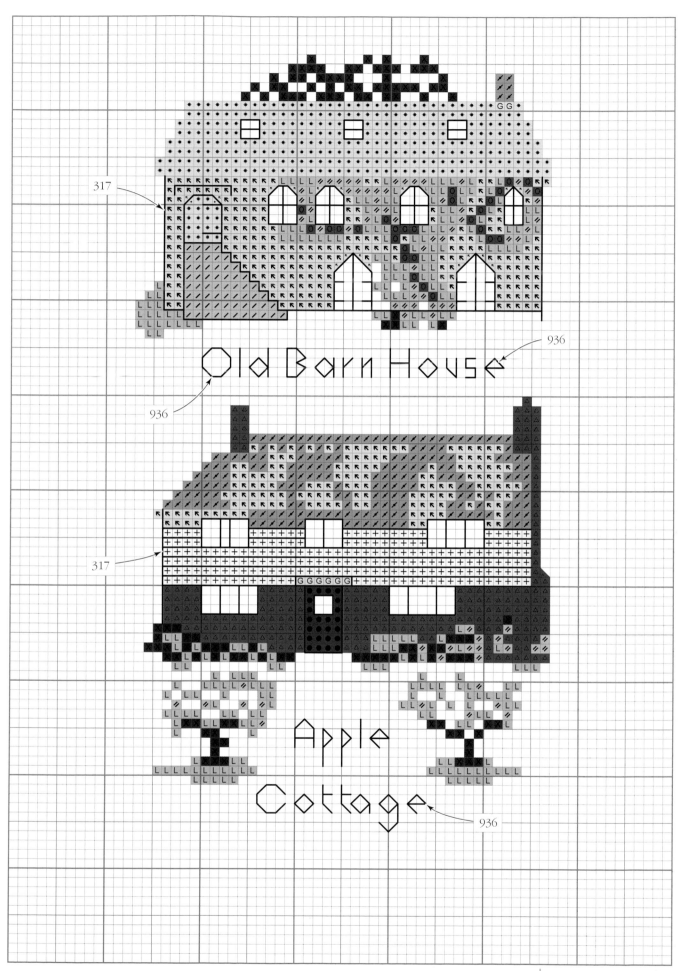

Old Barn House

Apple

Cottage

317

936

936

317

936

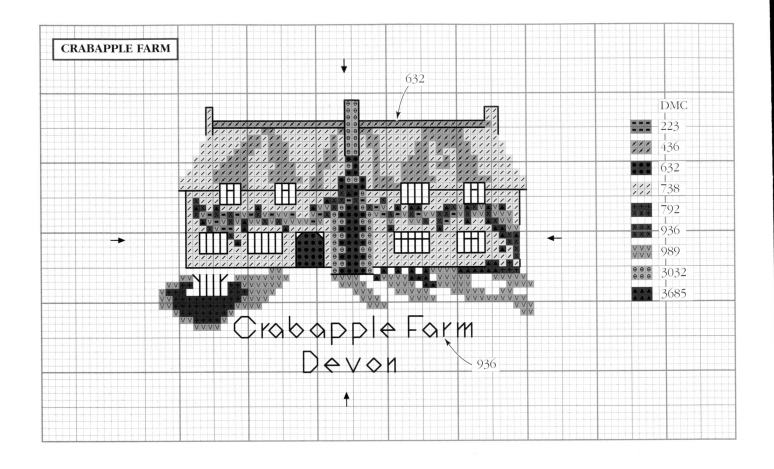

CRABAPPLE FARM

632

DMC	
▦▦▦	223
⁄⁄⁄	436
■■■	632
⁄⁄⁄	738
××	792
▨▨▨	936
∨∨∨	989
⊕⊕⊕	3032
▲▲▲	3685

Crabapple Farm
Devon

936

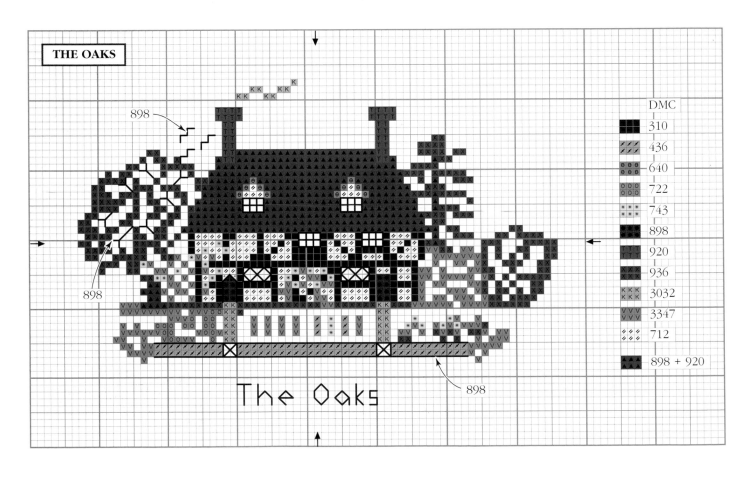

THE OAKS

898

898

898

DMC	
■■■	310
⁄⁄⁄	436
⊕⊕⊕	640
○○○	722
✴✴✴	743
■■■	898
TTT	920
▨▨▨	936
KKK	3032
∨∨∨	3347
⁄⁄⁄	712
▲▲▲	898 + 920

The Oaks

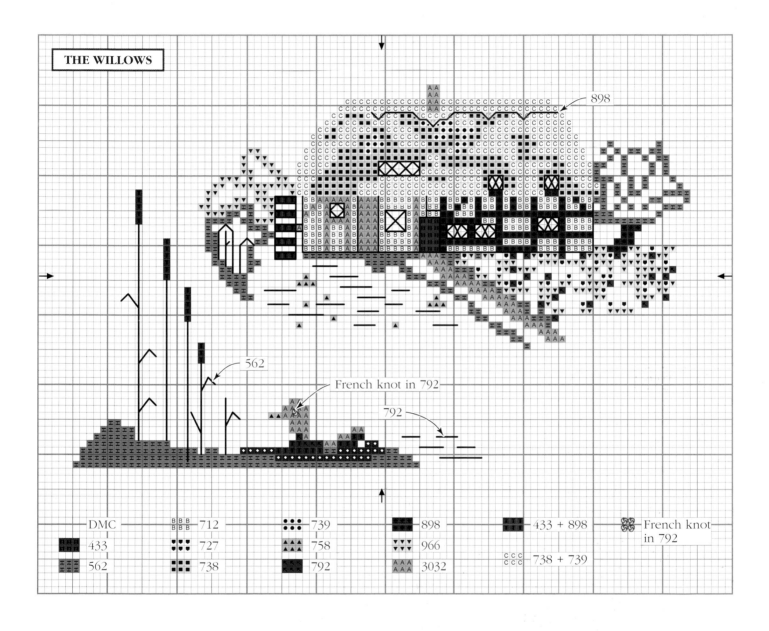

THE WILLOWS

898

562

French knot in 792

792

DMC					
433	712	739	898	433 + 898	French knot in 792
562	727	758	966	738 + 739	
	738	792	3032		

VICTORIAN COTTAGE BOOK COVER

*This pretty cottage design makes the perfect cover
for a diary or a gardener's notebook.*

Stitch count: 54 x 93

Design size: 17 x 9.5cm (6½ x 3¾in)

Refer to Quick Start page 11, and follow the chart opposite.

For the book cover shown, work on a 25.5 x 30.5cm (10 x 12in)
piece of 28-count antique white Cashel linen. Stitch over two fabric
threads, using two strands of stranded cotton (floss) for cross
stitches and then one strand to add the backstitches.

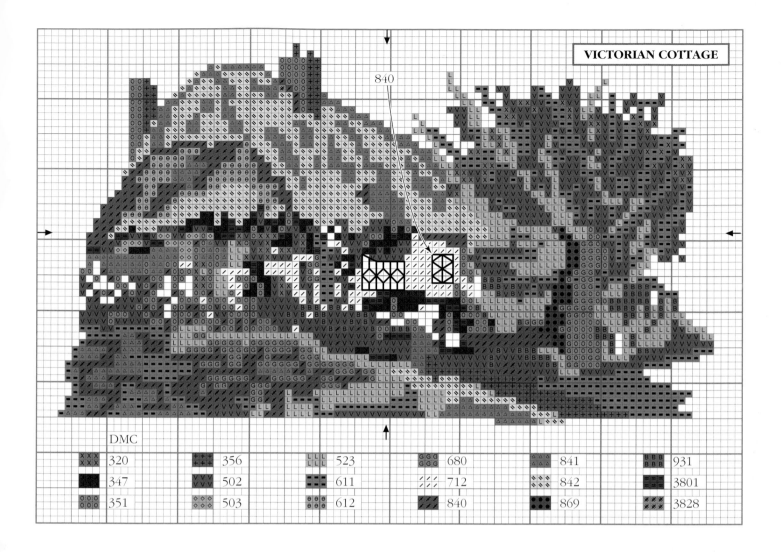

DMC							
320	356	523	680	841	931
347	502	611	712	842	3801
351	503	612	840	869	3828

Making up the book cover

You will need: 28-count antique white Cashel linen; firm card; polyester wadding (batting); lining fabric; matching sewing thread and twisted cord (see page 109).

To make up the book cover as shown, cut a piece of linen 25.5 x 30.5cm (10 x 12in) for the back cover and two pieces 23 x 5cm (9 x 2in) for the spine. Cut two pieces of firm card 20 x 25cm (8 x 10in) and one piece 25.2 x 2.5cm (10 x 1in) for the spine. Cut two pieces of polyester wadding (batting) slightly larger than the large card pieces and two pieces of lining fabric 25.5 x 30.5cm (10 x 12in) – see Fig 1 right.

Lay the embroidery face down on a clean surface, place a piece of wadding on top, then a piece of card. Fold the linen over the card and lace into position (see diagram page 108). Add the lining by folding in the raw edges, pinning in position and

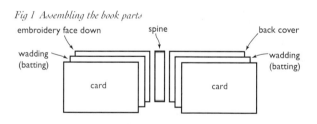

Fig 1 Assembling the book parts

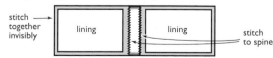

Fig 2 Slipstitching the covers and spine together

slipstitching to the embroidery. Make the back cover in the same way. Make the spine by covering the card with linen.

Place the front, spine and back pieces together (Fig 2), matching edges, and stitch together with strong thread. To finish, make a twisted cord from co-ordinating threads and tie around the spine.

COUNTRY SAMPLER

An idyllic English thatched cottage forms the focal point of this charming country sampler. I just love the little rabbits having a nibble in the corner and the butterflies that give it a real sense of summer. This design was originally stitched using Flower Threads, however, this single-ply matt thread is no longer generally available so the whole design has been re-charted in DMC stranded cotton (floss), although you could of course refer to the Anchor conversion chart on page 110 if you prefer to work in Anchor colours. The simple traditional alphabet and carnation border were charted from one of my antique samplers.

Stitch count: 131 x 177

Design size: 24 x 32cm (9½ x 12½in)

Refer to Quick Start page 11,
and follow the chart overleaf.

Work on 28-count antique white Cashel linen over two fabric threads, using two strands of stranded cotton (floss) for whole and three-quarter cross stitches. After all the cross stitch is completed, use one strand to add the backstitches in the colours given on the chart. If desired you could add more texture to the embroidery by stitching French knots using two strands of DMC 335 and 937 to the climbing plants on the front of the cottage. Once all stitching is complete, check for missed stitches and then mount and frame your sampler as preferred.

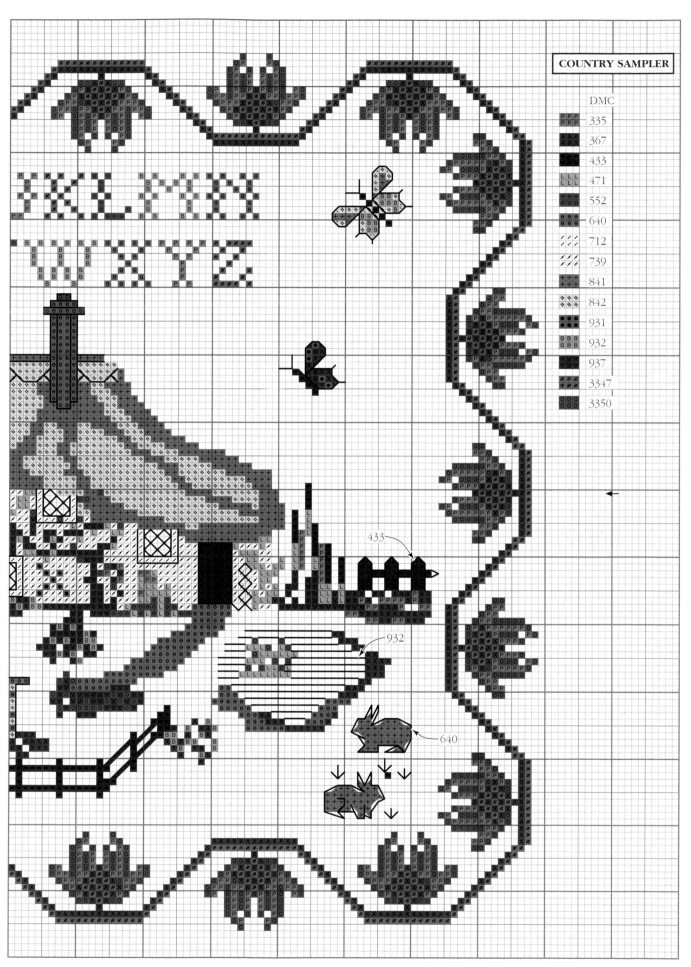

DMC
335
367
433
471
552
640
712
739
841
842
931
932
937
3347
3350

433

932

640

HAYSTACKS

I love this project. When I drew it (in the days of graph paper and pen) I could see just how it was going to look when stitched. You will see some variation between the chart and the original stitching which could not be avoided. The thread used for this design was a specialist space-dyed pure silk thread that is, sadly, no longer made. The chart has been redrawn using DMC stranded cotton (floss), adding a few glass beads for effect. The ivy makes a dramatic border for this cottage, covered in wisteria, ivy and roses.

Stitch count: 95 x 163

Design size: 17 x 29.5cm (6¾ x 11½in)

Additional requirements:
Mill Hill glass seed beads in green 03037
and red 72012

Refer to Quick Start page 11,
and follow the chart overleaf.

Work on 28-count antique white Cashel linen over two fabric threads using two strands of stranded cotton (floss) for whole and three-quarter cross stitches. After the cross stitch, use one strand to add the backstitches in the colours given on the chart. Add the glass seed beads with one strand of matching thread, a beading needle and a half cross stitch. Once all stitching is complete, check for missed stitches and then mount and frame as preferred.

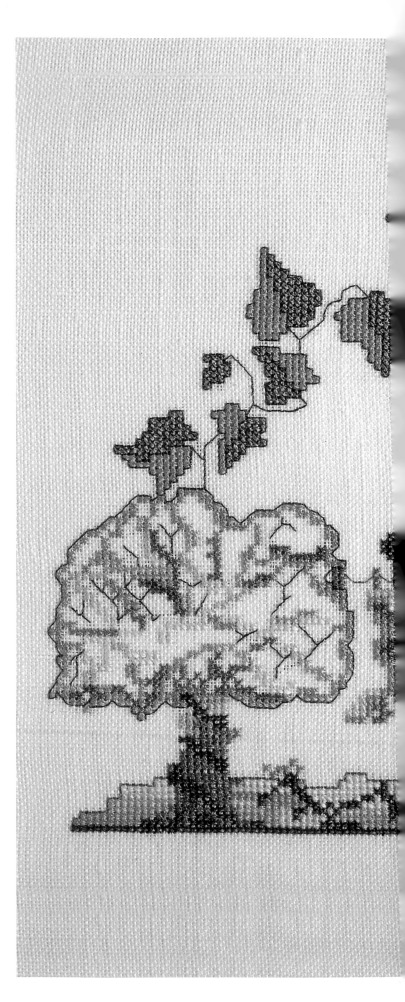

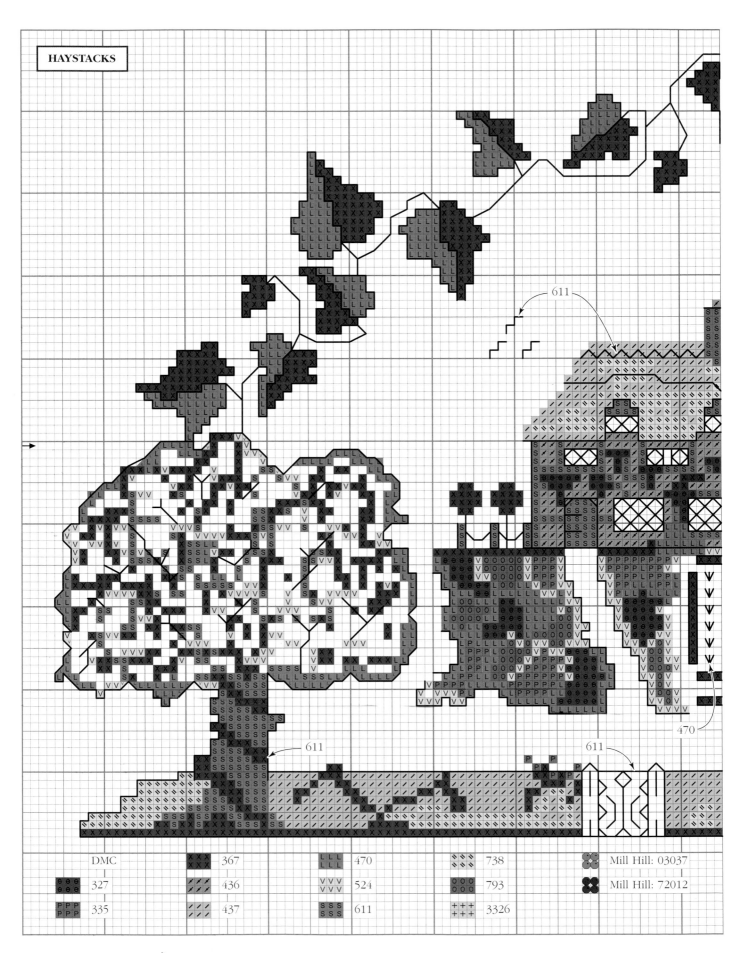

DMC			367			470			738	Mill Hill: 03037
327			436			524			793	Mill Hill: 72012
335			437			611			3326	

367

611

611

367

470

611

THERE'S NO PLACE LIKE HOME

This nostalgic project was inspired by my first purchase of embroidery on stitching paper. I know that this saying and 'Home Sweet Home' have become rather clichéd today and it is certainly included in cross stitch kits more often than any other, but I still love it. The original words are from the song 'Home, Sweet Home' written by J. H. Payne in 1822 (performed in the opera Clari, the Maid of Milan).

'Mid pleasures and palaces though we may roam,
Be it ever so humble,
There's no place like home.'

Stitch count: 143 x 217

Design size: 26 x 40cm (10¼ x 15½in)

Refer to Quick Start page 11,
and follow the chart overleaf.

Work on 28-count antique Cashel linen over two fabric threads using two strands of stranded cotton (floss) for cross stitches. After the cross stitch, use one strand to add the backstitches in the colours given on the chart. Work the backstitched decorative scrolls with two strands. Once all stitching is complete, mount and frame as preferred.

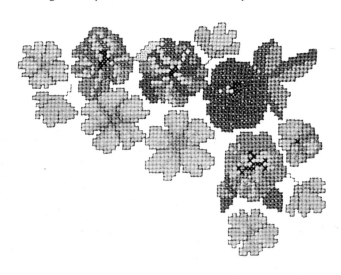

3740

3740

3740

327

327

3051

327

THERE'S NO PLACE LIKE HOME

	DMC
■	310
◐	327
◇	340
+	722
✳	725
Y	744
L	3042
✕	3051
V	3053
P	3688
▨	3740

3740

Fantastic Florals

As always, flowers are probably
the most popular cross stitchers'
topic and as I am a self-confessed cross
stitch addict, I am no exception. My only
difficulty was deciding which of my
favourites to include and which to leave
out! The flowers in this section of the book
tend to be of two main types – Berlin-style
patterns and stylized flowers drawn using a
backstitch outline. All of these designs may
be worked on 14-count Aida or 28-count
evenweave according to your preference.

ARUM LILY

The beautiful arum lily, with its arrow-shaped flowers and its broad, glossy green leaves, makes a wonderful picture on its own, or as a pair with the equally stunning golden lily, below.

Stitch count: 147 x 116

Design size: 26.5 x 21cm (10½ x 8¼in)

Additional requirements: Marlitt six-strand rayon in cream

Refer to Quick Start page 11, and follow the chart overleaf.

Work on 28-count unbleached Cashel linen over two fabric threads, using two strands of stranded cotton (floss) for cross stitches and French knots. Use two strands of Marlitt thread. After the cross stitch, use one strand to add the backstitch outlines and two strands for the backstitch lettering. Once all stitching is complete, mount and frame as preferred.

GOLDEN LILY

Both of these gorgeous lilies were copied from hand-coloured illustrations found in a book at the Natural History Museum in London.

Stitch count: 140 x 110

Design size: 25.5 x 20cm (10 x 8in)

Additional requirements: Marlitt six-strand rayon in bright yellow and orange

Refer to Quick Start page 11, and follow the chart on pages 84–85.

Work on 28-count unbleached Cashel linen over two fabric threads, using two strands of stranded cotton (floss) for cross stitches and French knots. Use two strands of Marlitt thead. After the cross stitch, use one strand to add the backstitch outlines and two strands for backstitch lettering. Once all stitching is complete, mount and frame as preferred.

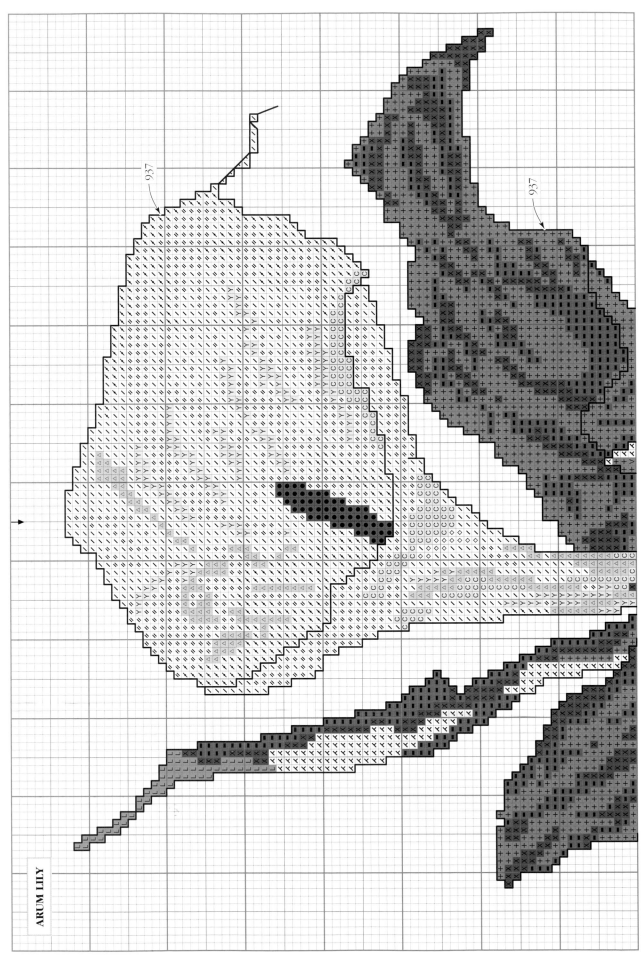

937

937

ARUM LILY

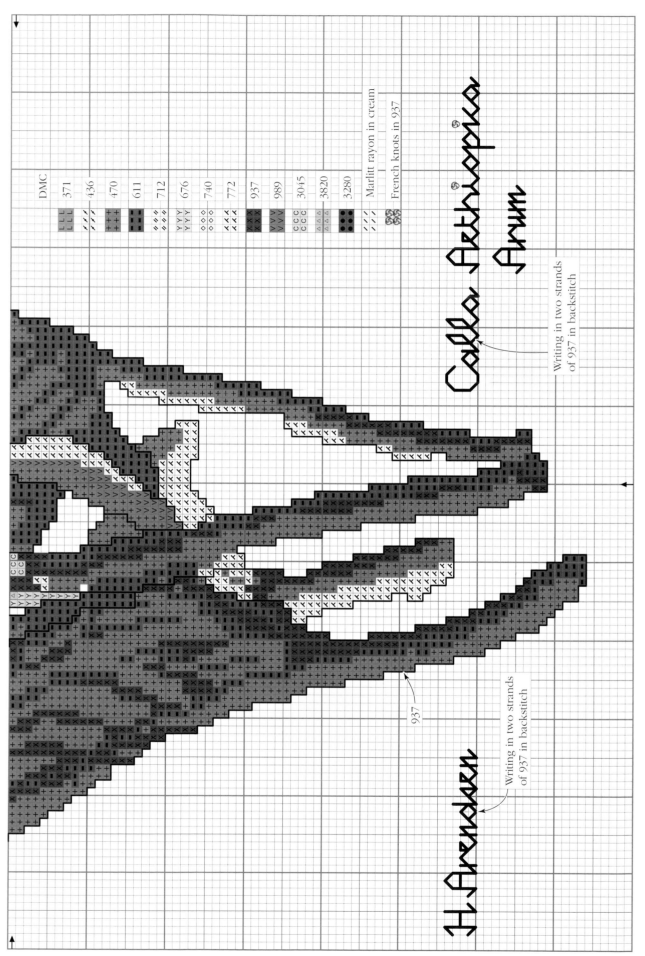

DMC			
371	L L L	L L L	
436	✓ ✓ ✓	✓ ✓ ✓	
470	+ + +	+ + +	
611	▮ ▮ ▮	▮ ▮ ▮	
712	∾ ∾ ∾	∾ ∾ ∾	
676	Y Y Y	Y Y Y	
740	◇ ◇ ◇	◇ ◇ ◇	
772	✗ ✗ ✗	✗ ✗ ✗	
937	✖ ✖ ✖	✖ ✖ ✖	
989	V V V	V V V	
3045	C C C	C C C	
3820	△ △ △	△ △ △	
3280	● ●	● ●	
Marlitt rayon in cream	⁄ ⁄ ⁄	⁄ ⁄ ⁄	
French knots in 937	✿ ✿		

Calla Aethiopica
Arum

Writing in two strands
of 937 in backstitch

937

H. Arendsen

Writing in two strands
of 937 in backstitch

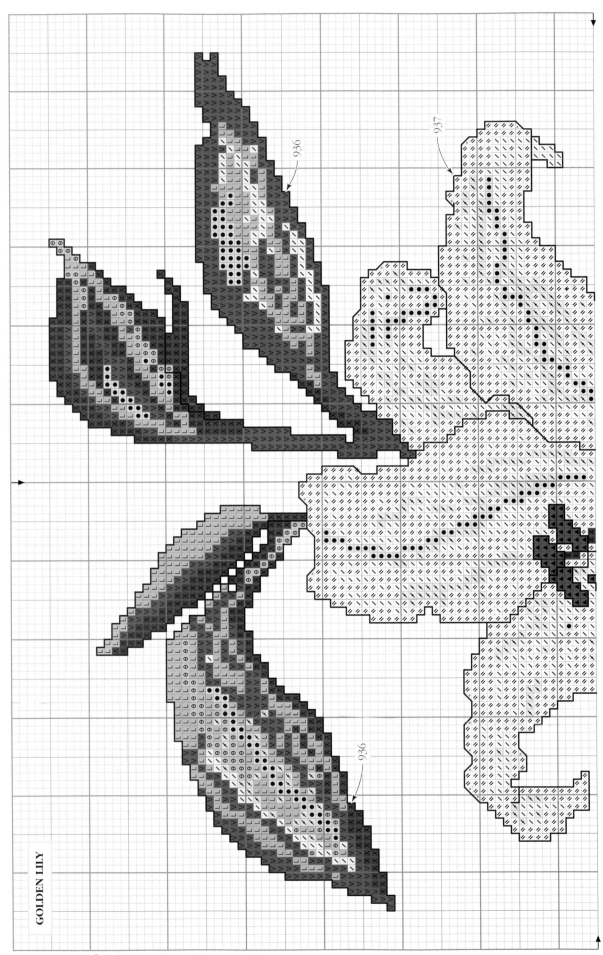

GOLDEN LILY

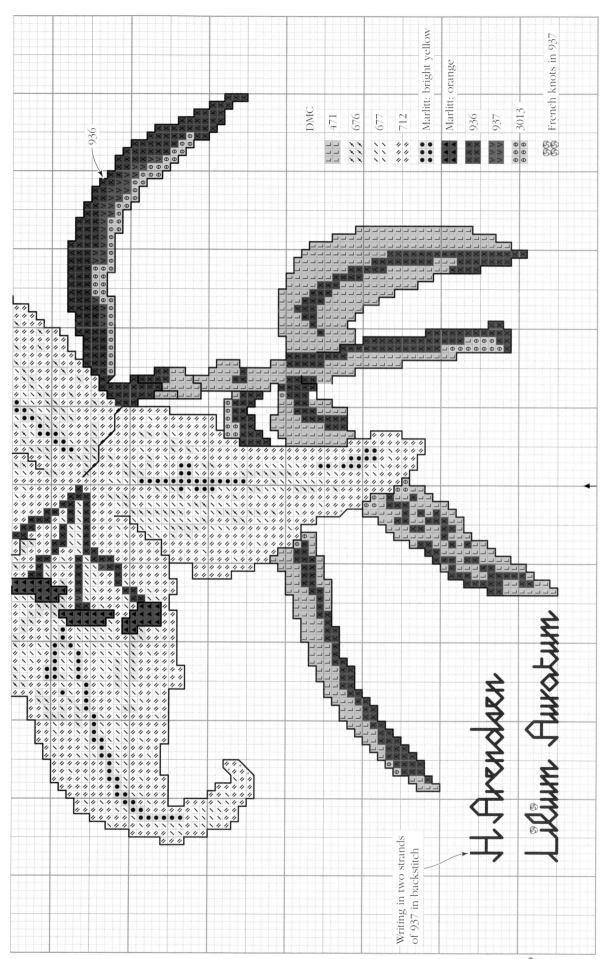

936

DMC			
471			
676			
677			
712			
Marlitt: bright yellow			
Marlitt: orange			
936			
937			
3013			
French knots in 937			

Writing in two strands
of 937 in backstitch

H. Arendsen
Lilium Auratum

POPPY APRON AND PAN HOLDER

Here is a chance to make something useful and practical. This apron and pan holder decorated with colourful poppies would grace any kitchen.

Apron stitch count: 67 x 76

Design size: 12 x 14cm (4¾ x 5½in)

Pan holder stitch count: 50 x 40

Design size: 9 x 7.25cm (3½ x 2¾in)

Refer to Quick Start page 11, follow the charts opposite and making up overleaf.

To stitch the apron motif, begin by creating the apron shape from a piece of 92 x 76cm (36 x 30in) 14-count pale green Aida fabric using the dimensions given in the diagram on page 88. Stitch the poppy motif on the apron in the position of your choice, working over one block of the Aida fabric and using two strands of stranded cotton (floss) for whole and three-quarter cross stitches. The blue bow is tweeded in two colours (see page 8). After the cross stitch, use one strand to add the backstitches in the colours given on the chart. See page 88 for making up instructions.

To stitch the pan holder motif, begin by cutting two pieces of 14-count light green Aida 104 x 24cm (41 x 9½in) and sewing a line of tacking (basting) thread 23cm (9in) from the short edge on each piece (see Fig 1 on page 88). Stitch the poppy sprays over one block of Aida in the centre of the marked squares, using two strands of stranded cotton (floss) for cross stitches and one strand for backstitches. See page 88 for making up instructions.

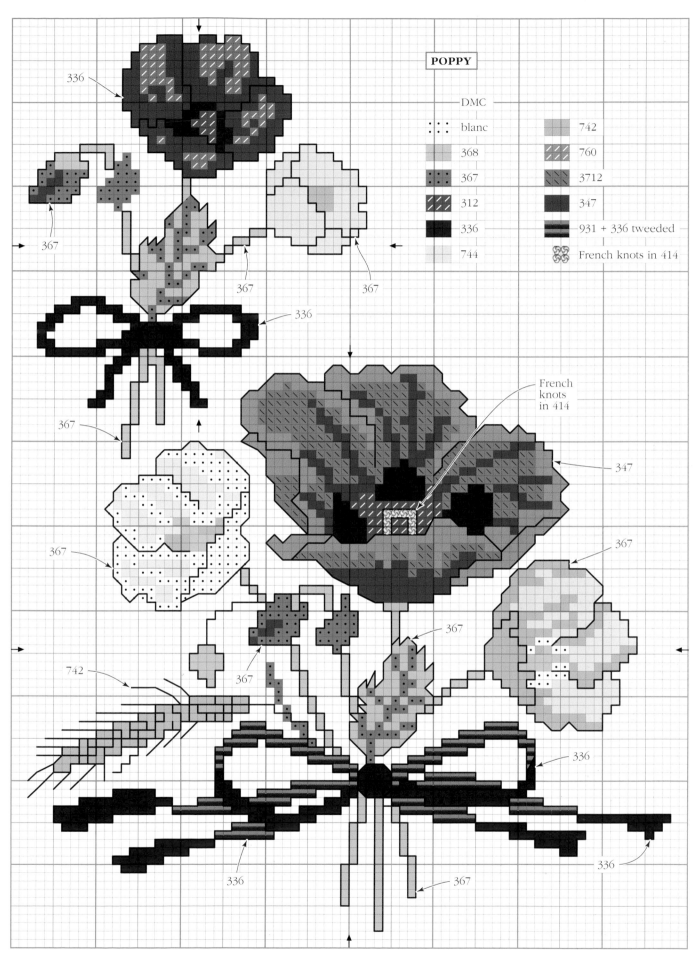

POPPY

DMC

blanc	
368	
367	
312	
336	
744	

742	
760	
3712	
347	
931 + 336 tweeded	
French knots in 414	

336

367

367

367

367

336

367

367

347

French knots in 414

367

742

336

336

336

367

Making up the apron

Bind around all the edges with home-made or ready-made bias binding (see page 109), adding ties for the neck and waist as you stitch. If adding a pocket, bind these edges too, and then top stitch the pocket to the front of the apron.

Apron and pocket pattern dimensions

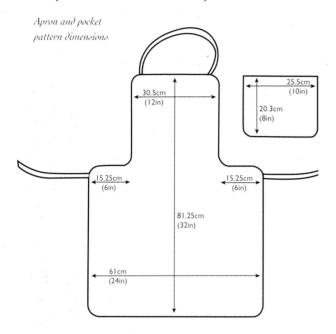

Making up the pan holder

You will need: polyester wadding (batting); blanket-weight fabric; lining fabric; bias binding and matching sewing thread.

Lay the finished embroidery right side down, cut polyester wadding (batting) the same size as the Aida shape and place on top. Cut two 23cm (9in) squares of blanket-weight fabric and place on top of the wadding, with one edge aligned with the tacking (basting) threads (see Fig 2, right). Tack (baste) in position around all four sides.

Cut a piece of lining fabric 104 x 24cm (41 x 9½in) and lay on top of the padded shape, then tack (baste) around the edge, through all layers.

Attach home-made or ready-made bias binding (see page 109) to the short edges and press lightly. Fold the bound edge on the line of the tacking (basting) and pin in position (see Fig 3, right). Now bind the two long edges, folding in raw edges. Remove tacking (basting) and press lightly to finish.

FOUR SEASON HEARTS

This quartet of seasonal hearts makes a lovely grouping on a wall. The spring heart has daffodils and pansies, the summer heart has honeysuckle and roses, the autumn heart has acorns and horse chestnuts, and the winter heart has holly and ivy.

Stitch count: 53 x 53 (approx each heart)

Design size: 10 x 10cm (4 x 4in)

Refer to Quick Start page 11, and follow the charts overleaf.

Work on 28-count antique white Cashel linen over two fabric threads, using two strands of stranded cotton (floss) for whole and three-quarter cross stitches. Use one strand to add the backstitches and long stitches in the colours on the chart. Mount and frame to finish.

Fig 1 Positions of the pan holder cross stitch motifs

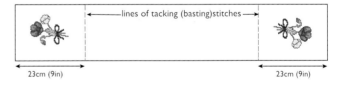

Fig 2 Layering the pan holder

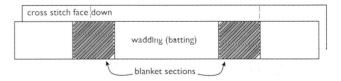

Fig 3 Stitching together and binding the pan holder

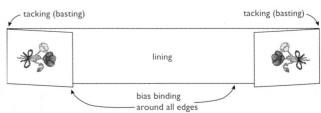

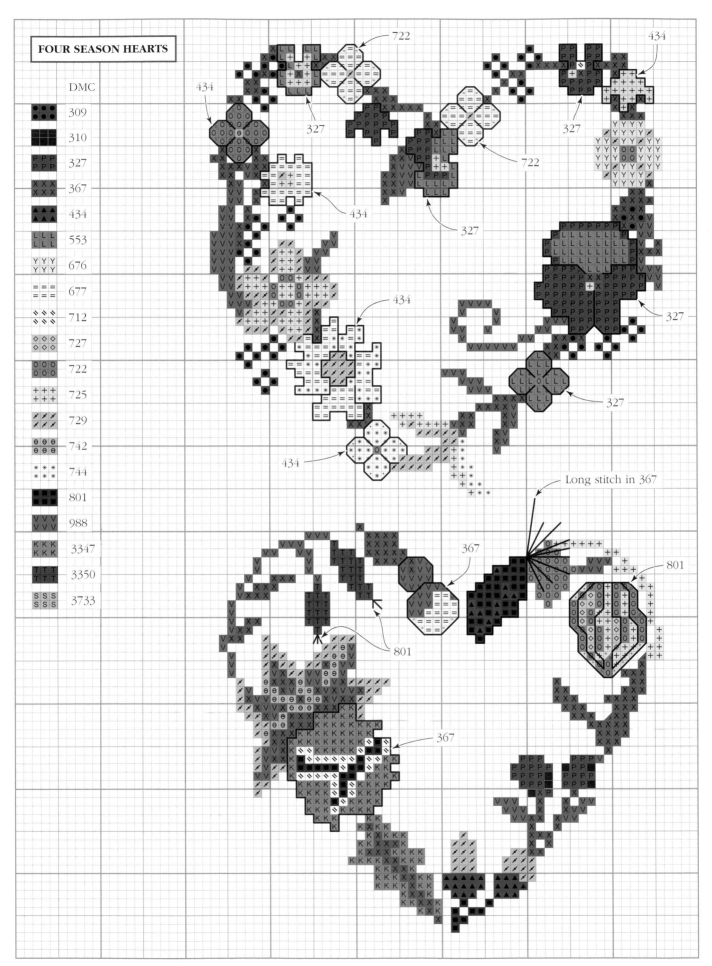

FOUR SEASON HEARTS

	DMC
●●	309
■■	310
PPP	327
XXX	367
▲▲	434
LLL	553
YYY	676
===	677
◊◊◊	712
◇◇◇	727
OOO	722
+++	725
⁄⁄⁄	729
θθθ	742
***	744
■■	801
VVV	988
KKK	3347
TTT	3350
SSS	3733

722

434

434

327

722

434

327

434

434

801

434

327

327

367

367

Long stitch in 367

801

367

801

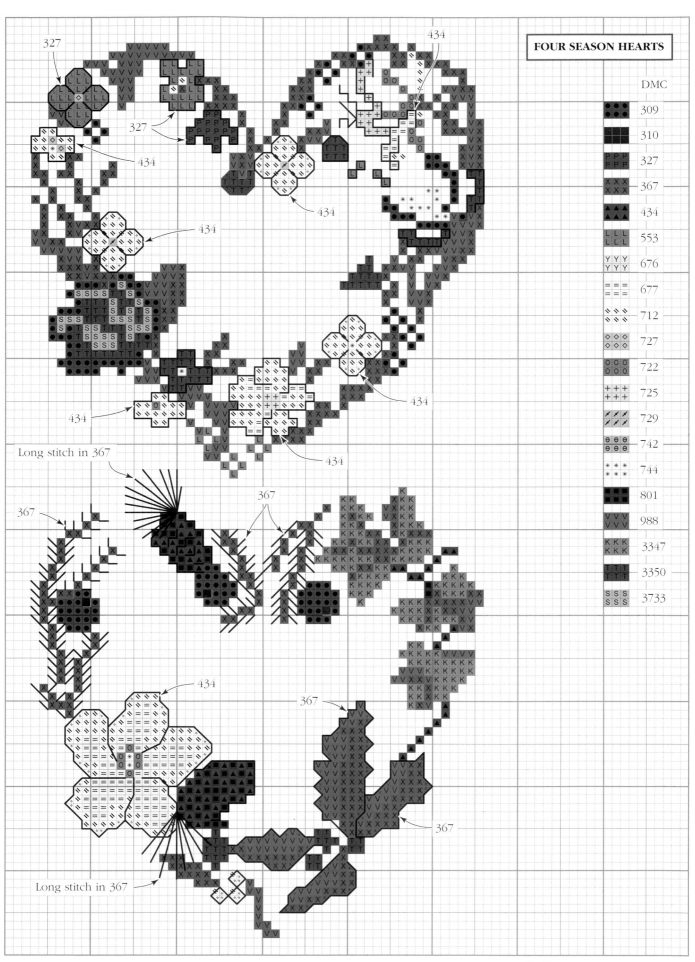

FOUR SEASON HEARTS

	DMC
●● 309
■■ 310
P P P 327
X X X 367
▲▲ 434
L L L 553
Y Y Y 676
= = = 677
◊◊◊ 712
◇◇◇ 727
O O O 722
+ + + 725
⫽⫽ 729
θ θ θ 742
* * * 744
■■ 801
V V V 988
K K K 3347
T T T 3350
S S S 3733

327

434

434

327

434

434

434

434

434

Long stitch in 367

367

367

367

434

367

367

Long stitch in 367

VIOLET AND ROSE ALPHABET SAMPLER

This beautiful alphabet sampler is one of my favourite projects. It was inspired by a French sampler which I discovered in a local antique shop. I was quite unable to afford to buy the sampler, which would have swallowed a month's housekeeping, so I came home and drew my own version! I can remember doing the drawing as if it was yesterday – some designs just fall into place. This project can also be used to make gift cards for your friends and relations using the decorated letters singly or in pairs.

Stitch count: 167 x 119

Design size: 30.5 x 21.5cm (12 x 8½in)

Refer to Quick Start page 11,
and follow the chart overleaf.

Work on 28-count cream Cashel linen over two fabric threads, using two strands of stranded cotton (floss) for whole and three-quarter cross stitches. After the cross stitch, add the backstitches using one strand in the colours given on the chart. Once the sampler is completed, check for missed stitches and then mount and frame as desired.

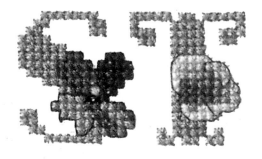

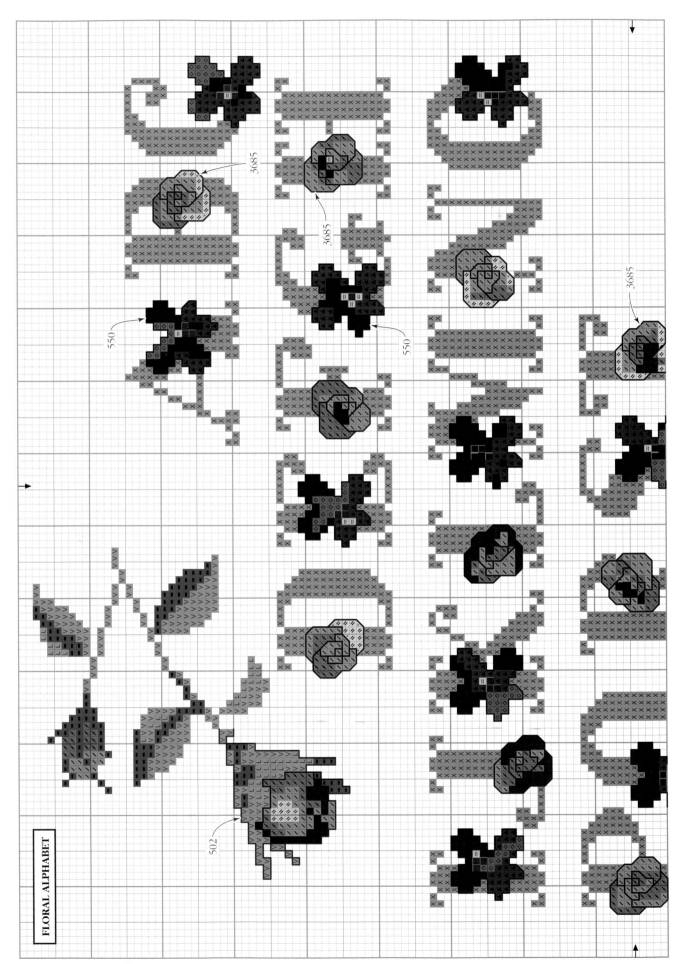

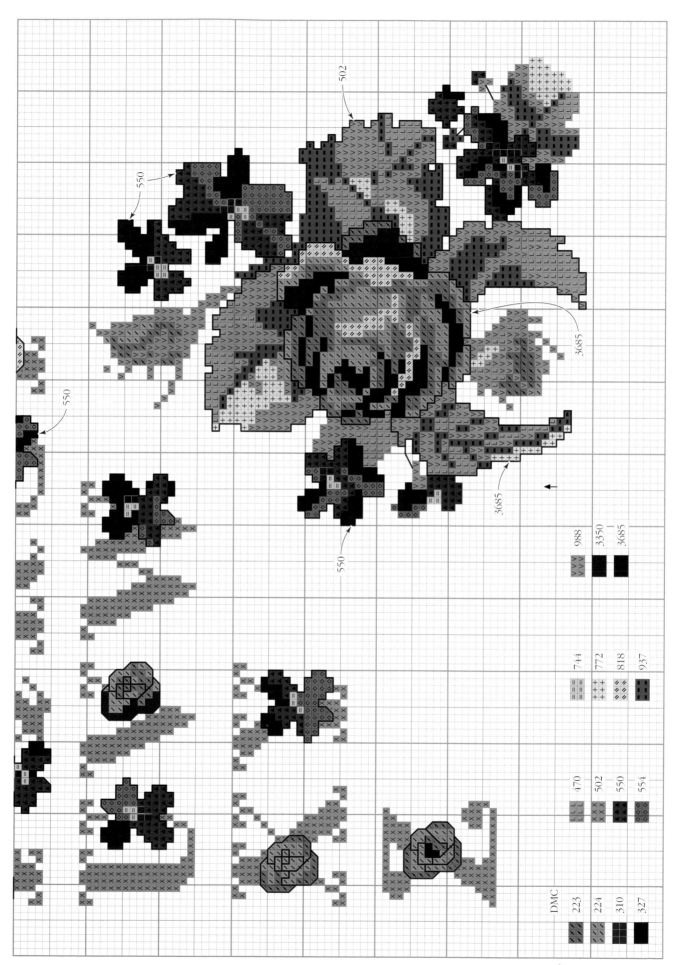

ROSE EVENING BAG

This sumptuous bag design comes from a Berlin chart, which I adapted to match a cerise-pink ball gown that I bought years ago. If you wanted to accessorize even further, you could also work a single flower from the design for a powder compact or handbag mirror.

Stitch count: 87 x 121

Design size: 16 x 22cm (6¼ x 8½in)

Refer to Quick Start page 11,
and follow the chart overleaf.

Work on 28-count cream Cashel linen over two fabric threads, using two strands of stranded cotton (floss) for cross stitches. The bag top shown here was found in a junk shop but you can purchase modern replicas (see Suppliers on page 111). The bag has an optional line of cross stitches to outline the shape. These are not shown on the chart as their positions will depend on the shape of your bag.

Making up the bag

You will need: 28-count cream Cashel linen for the bag back; cream lining fabric; interfacing (such as Vilene); a bag clasp/top; matching sewing thread and a length of twisted cord (see page 109).

Making up your evening bag will depend on the type of bag fastening you are using – these are general instructions for the type of bag shown opposite. Begin by making a paper pattern of your stitched piece, following the shape of the stitching and allowing 2cm (¾in) for turnings. Trim the embroidery to match the pattern and cut a similar piece of linen for the back of the bag and two pieces of lining fabric to match. Trim the paper pattern about 1.5cm (½in) all round and cut two pieces of interfacing (Vilene) to this shape.

On the wrong side of each linen shape lay a piece of interfacing, fold the turning allowance over and tack (baste) this into place (see Fig 1). Cut a strip of linen and lining fabric about 5cm (2in) wide for the gusset and attach to a piece of interfacing as described before.

Fig 1 Stitching the interfacing to the material

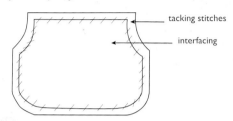

tacking stitches

interfacing

Stitch the front, gusset and back pieces together from the wrong side using matching sewing thread. Press on the wrong side and set aside. Stitch the front, back and gusset lining pieces together as above and press on the wrong side. With wrong sides together, stitch the lining section inside the bag section, matching seams.

Attach the handle to the bag according to the manufacturer's instructions. Purpose-made bag tops have small holes punched beneath the fitting, to which the needlework is stitched with small backstitches. In the bag shown, cream silk was used for the backstitch, which was then whipped (see Fig 2) to give the impression of a cord. Alternatively, you could cover the top edge of the lining with matching braid if you wish.

Fig 2 Whipping backstitch

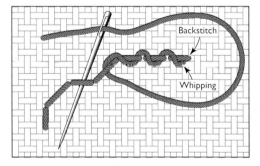

Backstitch

Whipping

A twisted cord for a handle makes a nice finishing touch. To make a length of cord, use threads that co-ordinate with your embroidery and follow the instructions on page 109. Alternatively, you can buy a length of toning ready-made cord.

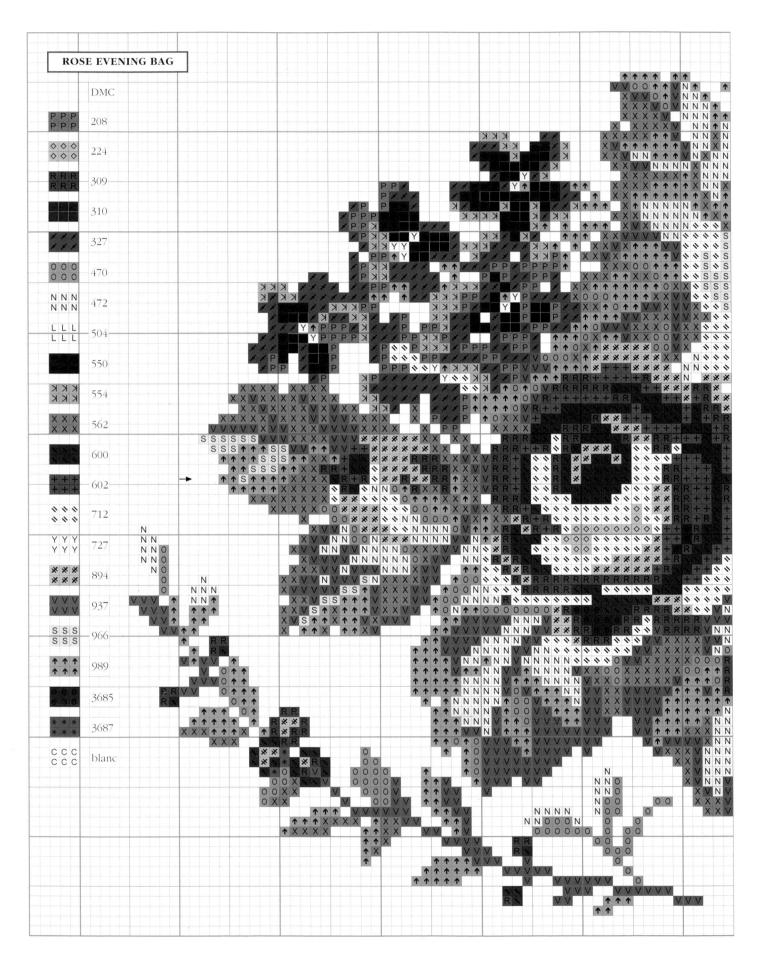

ROSE EVENING BAG

	DMC
P P P / P P P	208
◇ ◇ ◇ / ◇ ◇ ◇	224
R R R / R R R	309
	310
/ / /	327
O O O / O O O	470
N N N / N N N	472
L L L / L L L	504
	550
✕ ✕ ✕	554
X X X	562
V V V / V V V	562
S S S / S S S	600
+ + +	602
◇ ◇ ◇	712
Y Y Y / Y Y Y	727
✻ ✻ ✻	894
V V V / V V V	937
S S S / S S S	966
↑ ↑ ↑ / ↑ ↑ ↑	989
❂ ❂ ❂	3685
✳ ✳ ✳	3687
C C C / C C C	blanc

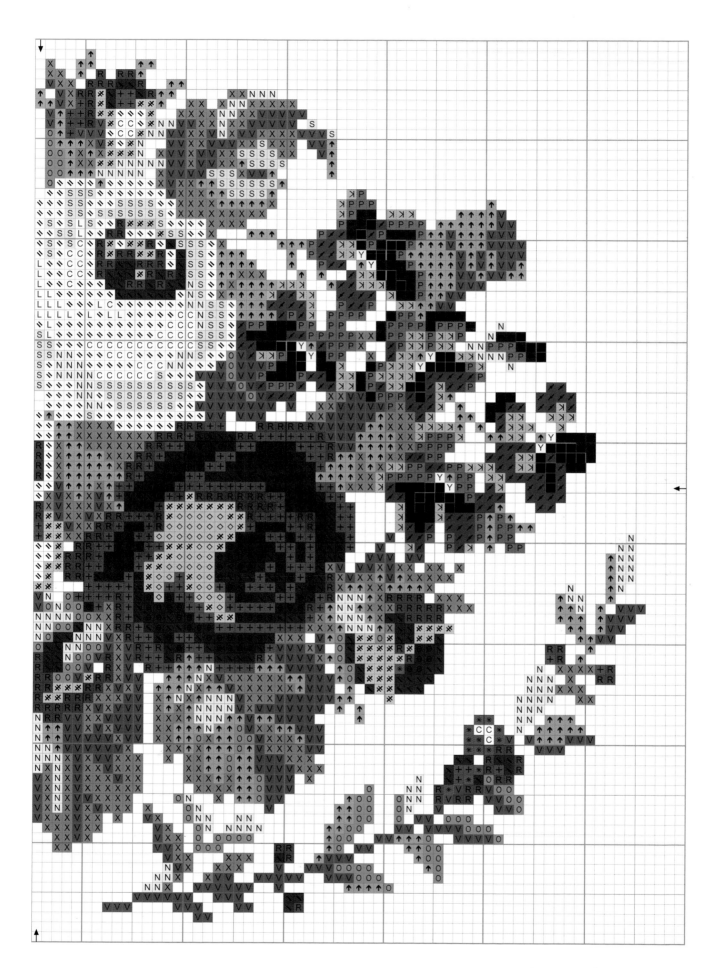

WATER LILY CUSHION

These evocative lilies could be made as a picture but I love the effect they have on this cushion.

Stitch count: 72 x 98

Design size: 13 x 18cm (5¼ x 7in)

Refer to Quick Start page 11,
and follow the chart opposite.

Work on 14-count cream damask Aida over one block using two strands of stranded cotton (floss) for cross stitches. The long blue stitches around the flower represent water and are worked in rows of half cross stitch only. After the cross stitch add the backstitches using one strand. Make up as a mitred cushion following the instructions on page 109.

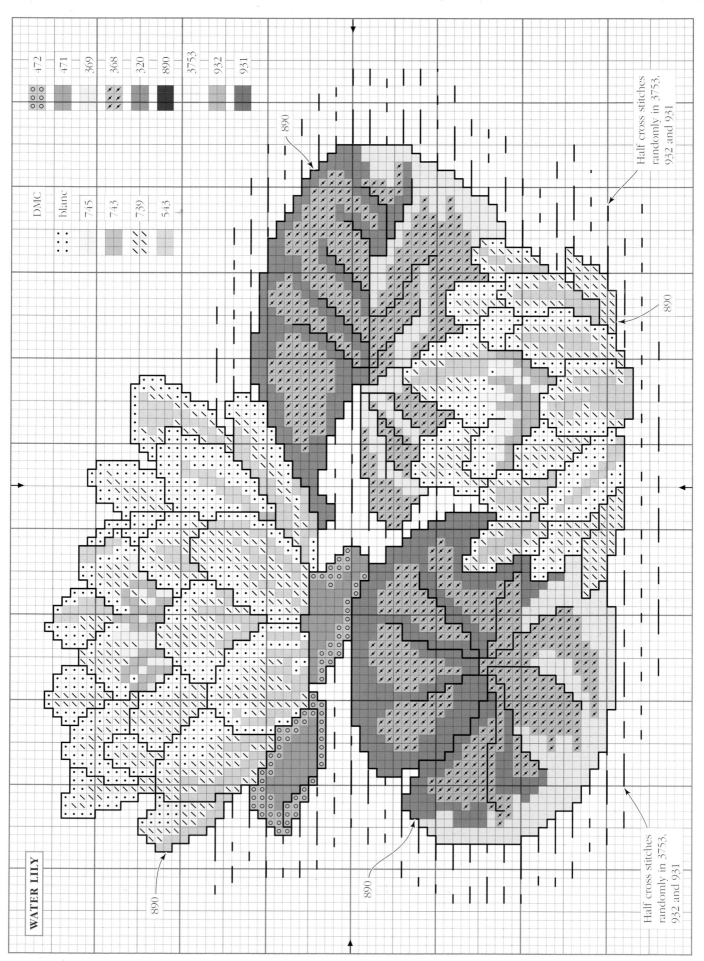

WATER LILY

		472	471	369	368	320	890	3753	932	931

DMC	blanc	745	743	739	543

890

890

890

890

Half cross stitches randomly in 3753, 932 and 931

Half cross stitches randomly in 3753, 932 and 931

ROSEBUD CUSHION

I found this gorgeous Victorian Garland design in a folder of original Berlin patterns whilst viewing at a saleroom. If you prefer, it would make a lovely footstool pattern instead of a cushion. Your local craft shop should have various wooden footstool designs in stock, or refer to needlework magazines for mail-order companies.

Stitch count: 100 x 121

Design size: 18 x 22cm (7 x 8½in)

Refer to Quick Start page 11, and follow the chart opposite.

Work on 28-count cream Cashel linen over two fabric threads, using two strands of stranded cotton (floss) for cross stitches. Make up as a mitred cushion following the instructions on page 109.

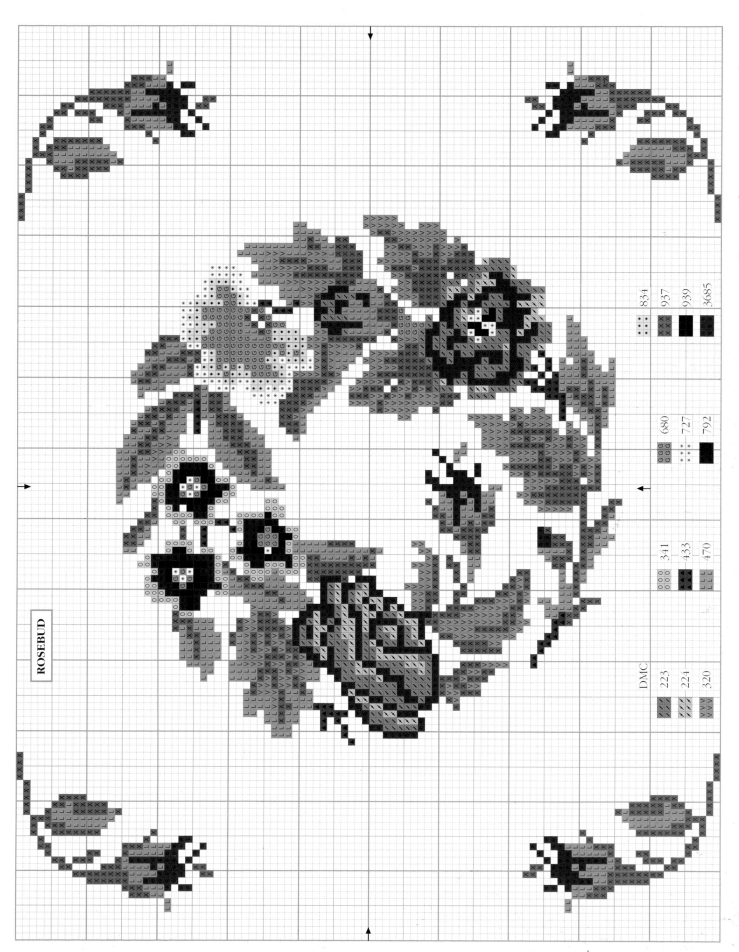

ROSEBUD

DMC					
223	341	680	834		
224	433	727	937		
320	470	792	939		
			3685		

ROSE HEART PINCUSHION

This charming little design is quick to stitch and perfect for use on other items, such as cards, coasters and trinket pot lids.

Stitch count: 41 x 41

Design size: 7.5 x 7.5cm (3 x 3in)

Refer to Quick Start page 11,
and follow the chart opposite.

Work on 28-count cream Cashel linen over two threads using two strands of stranded cotton (floss) for cross stitches. Add the backstitches using one strand. Mount into a pincushion of your choice, following the manufacturer's instructions.

ROSE WREATH PINCUSHION

This design would also look very pretty made up into a scented sachet or special card, perhaps with a greeting backstitched in the centre.

Stitch count: 61 x 59

Design size: 11 x 10.75cm (4½ x 4¼in)

Refer to Quick Start page 11,
and follow the chart opposite.

Work on 28-count cream Cashel linen over two fabric threads using two strands of stranded cotton (floss) for cross stitches. Mount into a pincushion of your choice, following the manufacturer's instructions.

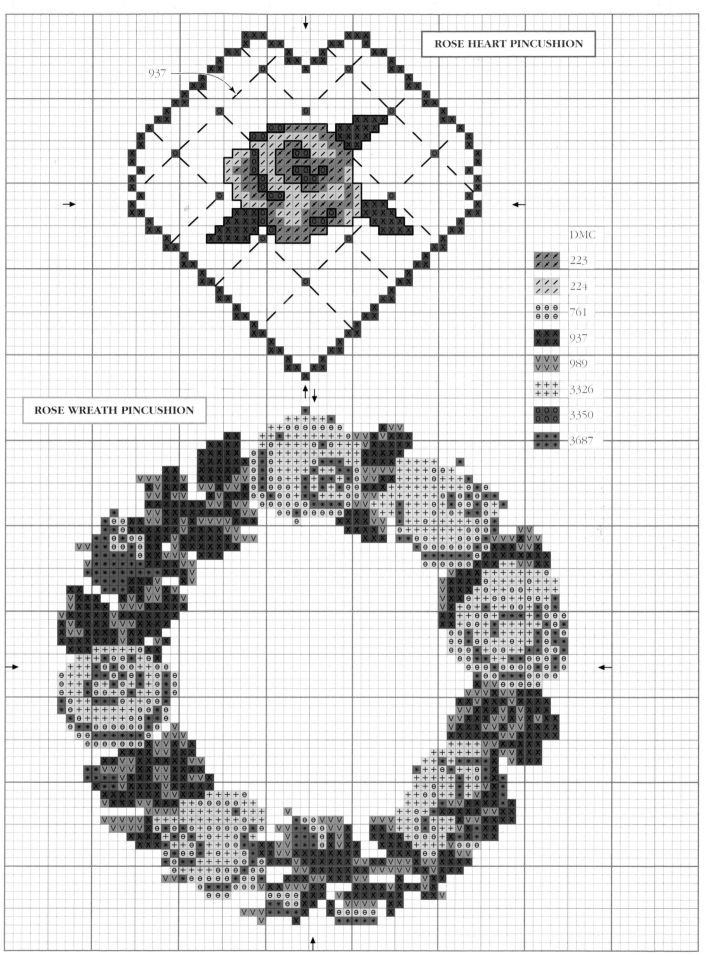

ROSE HEART PINCUSHION

937

ROSE WREATH PINCUSHION

	DMC
⁄⁄⁄	223
⁄⁄⁄	224
θθθ	761
XXX	937
VVV	989
+++	3326
ooo	3350
***	3687

PERSONALIZING THE DESIGNS

Alphabets and numerals are charted here to allow you to personalize the Beaded Lily Wedding Sampler on page 13, the Our Special Day Sampler on page 16 and the Lace Birth Sampler on page 24. When stitching your own names, dates and messages it is best to plan the letters and numbers out on graph paper first, to ensure the spacing looks pleasing and will fit the space available on the fabric before you begin to stitch.

Use this diagram when making up the Passion Flower Horseshoe on page 22. The half horseshoe shape is provided here actual size. Trace the shape on to tracing paper and transfer the design on to a large sheet of paper. Flip the tracing over to complete the whole horseshoe and then cut out the paper shape and use it as a pattern.

PASSION FLOWER HORSESHOE
Half horseshoe pattern

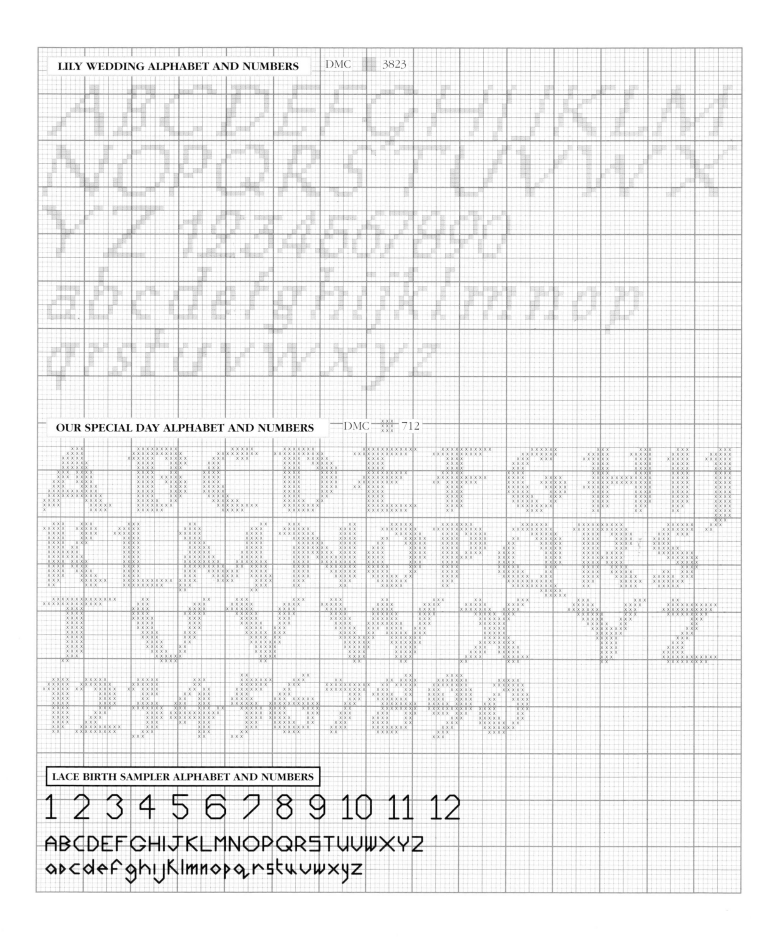

LILY WEDDING ALPHABET AND NUMBERS DMC 3823

OUR SPECIAL DAY ALPHABET AND NUMBERS DMC 712

LACE BIRTH SAMPLER ALPHABET AND NUMBERS

1 2 3 4 5 6 7 8 9 10 11 12

ABCDEFGHIJKLMNOPQRSTUVWXYZ

abcdefghijklmnopqrstuvwxyz

FINISHING AND MAKING UP

Your cross stitch embroidery can be made up into a wonderful range of items, both decorative and practical. This section describes some general finishing and making up techniques, including mounting work in cards, framing and creating cushions.

Mounting work in cards

There are many blank cards available from needlecraft shops and mail-order companies and the following method of mounting should suit most brands.

When stitching is complete, press the design on the wrong side – on thick towels to avoid flattening the stitches. Open the folded card and check that the design fits in the aperture. Apply a thin coat of adhesive or double-sided adhesive tape to the inside of the opening. Place the embroidery carefully into position, checking it is centred in the opening and then press down firmly. Fold the flap over the back of the embroidery, stick in place with double-sided tape or glue and leave to dry before closing. Add ribbon trims to the card as desired.

Stretching and mounting work

Professional framing can be expensive but we all feel our larger projects deserve the professional touch. By following the method explained below for padded mounting, you will be able to produce a very good result on your own. The advantage of a padded mounting for embroidery is that any slightly 'lumpy bits' on the back of your work will be pushed into the padding rather than appear as raised areas on the front.

You will need: 3mm foamcore board or acid-free mount board; double-sided tape or strong thread; polyester wadding (batting) and glass- or plastic-headed pins.

Using a sharp craft knife, cut a piece of foamcore to fit your frame (an easy way to do this is to cut round the piece of glass that fits the frame). Attach a piece of wadding (batting) to the foamcore using long strips

of double-sided tape, then trim the wadding to the same size as the foamcore.

Position your embroidery on top of the padding, centring it carefully. Now fix the embroidery into position by pinning through the fabric into the foamcore edges, starting in the middle of each side and pinning towards the corners. Make sure your pins follow a line of Aida holes or a linen thread so your edges are really straight. Adjust the fabric's position as necessary until you are completely confident that it is centred and straight.

Turn the work over and, leaving the pins in place, trim the excess fabric to about 5cm (2in) all round and then fold it to the back. Fix the edges of the fabric in place using either double-sided tape (see the first diagram below) or by lacing across the back using strong thread (as shown in the bottom diagram). As the pins remain in place, it is still possible at this stage to adjust the position of the fabric and replace the tape or tighten the lacing. When you are completely satisfied with the result, remove the pins and then assemble the mounted embroidery in your picture frame.

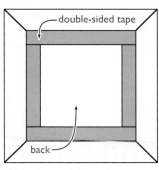
Mounting work by taping

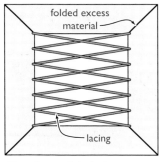
Mounting work by lacing

Framing work

There are many attractive ready-made frames available today from numerous stores, and if the frame isn't the best colour to complement your embroidery there are plenty of paints you can use to customize the frame.

Needlework generally looks better framed without glass. If you prefer to use glass you must ensure that the embroidery does not touch the underside of the glass. Insert very narrow strips of board (spacers) into the edges of the frame, between the glass and the mounted embroidery, to hold them apart before you assemble the frame. Always check that both sides of the glass are completely clean before assembling the frame. Before adding the final backing board to the back of the picture, line the back of the work with aluminium foil to discourage small insects.

Making cushions and pincushions

This is quite straightforward although two of the cushions in this book (see page 100 and 102) have been made a little more special by insetting the embroidery into a mitred front (described top of page 109).

For a basic cushion or pincushion, place the embroidered piece of fabric and a piece of backing fabric the same size wrong sides together and sew together around all sides, leaving a gap for turning. Turn through to the right side, insert a cushion pad or stuffing and then slipstitch the gap closed. The edges can be decorated with twisted cord (see page 109) or braid as desired.

Making a mitred cushion front

First measure your embroidery and decide on the size the finished cushion is to be. Allow 1.25cm (½in) for seam allowances. Subtract the embroidery measurement from the two finished measurements, divide by two and add on the two seam allowances. This gives the total width of the border pieces. The length of the border pieces is the finished measurement of the cushion cover plus two seam allowances.

Press the embroidery face down on several towels. Cut the embroidery fabric to the required size plus two seam allowances. Find the mid-point of each edge by folding and then mark with a pin. Fold each border panel in half to find the centre and mark with a pin. Pin the border panels to the embroidery, matching centre points and leaving the edges free. Machine stitch these seams around each side of the square, with seams meeting at the corners at right angles. Fold the embroidery in half diagonally, wrong sides together, and mitre the corners by stitching a line from the corner of the embroidery to the corner of the border panels (see diagram below).

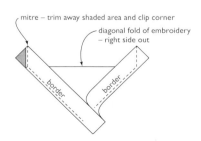

Mitring fabric on a cushion front

Trim the excess cloth and clip the corners. Repeat for the remaining corners and then make up as simple cushion as described on page 108, adding a frill if you wish.

Using bias binding

The poppy apron and pan holder on page 86 are edged with bias binding. You can use ready-made binding or make your own.

To make binding, cut fabric strips 4cm (1½in) wide across the grain and sew the strips together to make the length needed.

To attach bias binding, cut the binding to length, pin it to the wrong side of the project, matching raw edges, and stitch in place by hand or machine. Fold the binding to the right side and top stitch into position. Press lightly to finish.

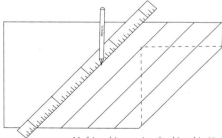

Making bias strips for bias binding

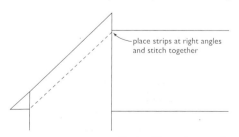

Sewing bias strips together

Making a twisted cord

Many embroidery projects are nicely finished off with a twisted cord. Choose a colour or group of colours in stranded cottons (floss) to match your embroidery and cut a minimum of four lengths, at least four times the finished length required. Fold in half and ask a friend to hold the two ends, whilst you slip a pencil through the loop at the other end. Twist the pencil and keep twisting until kinks appear. Walk slowly towards your partner and the cord will automatically twist. Smooth out the kinks from the looped end and tie another knot at the other end to secure. The cord can then be slipstitched into place.

DMC-ANCHOR THREAD CONVERSION CHART

This thread conversion chart is only a guide as exact colour comparisons cannot always be made.
An * indicates an Anchor shade used more than once, so take care to avoid duplication. If you wish to use
Madeira threads, telephone for a conversion chart on 01765 640003 or email: acts@madeira.co.uk

DMC	ANCHOR	DMC	ANCHOR	DMC	ANCHOR	DMC	ANCHOR	DMC	ANCHOR	DMC	ANCHOR	DMC	ANCHOR	DMC	ANCHOR
		353	8*	603	62*	780	309	911	205	3022	8581*	3761	928	3845	1089*
B 5200	1	355	1014	604	55	781	308*	912	209	3023	899	3765	170	3846	1090
White	2	356	1013*	605	1094	782	308*	913	204	3024	388*	3766	167	3847	1076*
Ecru	387*	367	216	606	334	783	307	915	1029	3031	905*	3768	779	3848	1074*
150	59	368	214	608	330*	791	178	917	89	3032	898*	3770	1009	3849	1070*
151	73	369	1043	610	889	792	941	918	341	3033	387*	3772	1007	3850	188*
152	969	370	888*	611	898*	793	176*	919	340	3041	871	3773	1008	3851	186*
153	95*	371	887*	612	832	794	175	920	1004	3042	870	3774	778	3852	306*
154	873	372	887*	613	831	796	133	921	1003*	3045	888*	3776	1048*	3853	1003*
155	1030*	400	351	632	936	797	132	922	1003*	3046	887*	3777	1015	3854	313
156	118*	402	1047*	640	393	798	146	924	851	3047	887	3778	1013*	3855	311*
157	120*	407	914	642	392	799	145	926	850	3051	845*	3779	868	3856	347
158	178	413	236*	644	391	800	144	927	849	3052	844	3781	1050	3857	936*
159	120*	414	235*	645	273	801	359	928	274	3053	843	3782	388*	3858	1007
160	175*	415	398	646	8581*	806	169	930	1035	3064	883	3787	904*	3859	914*
161	176	420	374	647	1040	807	168	931	1034	3072	397	3790	904*	3860	379*
162	159*	422	372	648	900	809	130	932	1033	3078	292	3799	236*	3861	378
163	877	433	358	666	46	813	161*	934	852*	3325	129	3801	1098	3862	358*
164	240*	434	310	676	891	814	45	935	861	3326	36	3802	1019*	3863	379*
165	278*	435	365	677	361*	815	44	936	846	3328	1024	3803	69	3864	376
166	280*	436	363	680	901*	816	43	937	268*	3340	329	3804	63*	3865	2*
167	375*	437	362	699	923*	817	13*	938	381	3341	328	3805	62*	3866	926*
168	274*	444	291	700	228	818	23*	939	152*	3345	268*	3806	62*	48	1207
169	849*	445	288	701	227	819	271	943	189	3346	267*	3807	122	51	1220*
208	110	451	233	702	226	820	134	945	881	3347	266*	3808	1068	52	1209*
209	109	452	232	703	238	822	390	946	332	3348	264	3809	1066*	57	1203*
210	108	453	231	704	256*	823	152*	947	330*	3350	77	3810	1066*	61	1218*
211	342	469	267*	712	926	824	164	948	1011	3354	74	3811	1060	62	1202*
221	897*	470	266*	718	88	825	162*	950	4146	3362	263	3812	188	67	1212
223	895	471	265	720	326	826	161*	951	1010	3363	262	3813	875*	69	1218*
224	895	472	253	721	324	827	160	954	203*	3364	261	3814	1074	75	1206*
225	1026	498	1005	722	323*	828	9159	955	203*	3371	382	3815	877*	90	1217*
300	352	500	683	725	305*	829	906	956	40*	3607	87	3816	876*	91	1211
301	1049*	501	878	726	295*	830	277*	957	50	3608	86	3817	875*	92	1215*
304	19	502	877*	727	293	831	277*	958	187	3609	85	3818	923*	93	1210*
307	289	503	876*	729	890	832	907*	959	186	3685	1028	3819	278	94	1216
309	42	504	206*	730	845*	833	874*	961	76*	3687	68	3820	306	95	1209*
310	403	517	162*	731	281*	834	874*	962	75*	3688	75*	3821	305*	99	1204
311	148	518	1039	732	281*	838	1088	963	23*	3689	49	3822	295*	101	1213*
312	979	519	1038	733	280	839	1086	964	185	3705	35*	3823	386	102	1209*
315	1019*	520	862*	734	279	840	1084	966	240	3706	33*	3824	8*	103	1210*
316	1017	522	860	738	361*	841	1082	970	925	3708	31	3825	323*	104	1217*
317	400	523	859	739	366	842	1080	971	316*	3712	1023	3826	1049*	105	1218*
318	235*	524	858	740	316*	844	1041	972	298	3713	1020	3827	311	106	1203*
319	1044*	535	401	741	304	869	375	973	290	3716	25	3828	373	107	1203*
320	215	543	933	742	303	890	218	975	357	3721	896	3829	901*	108	1220*
321	47	550	101*	743	302	891	35*	976	1001	3722	1027	3830	5975	111	1218*
322	978	552	99	744	301	892	33*	977	1002	3726	1018	3831	29	112	1201*
326	59*	553	98	745	300	893	27	986	246	3727	1016	3832	28	113	1210*
327	101*	554	95	746	275	894	26	987	244	3731	76*	3833	31*	114	1213*
333	119	561	212	747	158	895	1044*	988	243	3733	75*	3834	100*	115	1206*
334	977	562	210	754	1012	898	380	989	242	3740	872	3835	98*	121	1210*
335	40*	563	208	758	9575	899	38	991	1076	3743	869	3836	90	122	1215*
336	150	564	206*	760	1022	900	333	992	1072	3746	1030	3837	100*	124	1210*
340	118	580	924	761	1021	902	897*	993	1070	3747	120	3838	177	125	1213*
341	117*	581	281*	762	234	904	258	995	410	3750	1036	3839	176*	126	1209*
347	1025	597	1064	772	259*	905	257	996	433	3752	1032	3840	120*		
349	13*	598	1062	775	128	906	256*	3011	856	3753	1031	3841	159*		
350	11	600	59*	776	24	907	255	3012	855	3755	140	3842	164*		
351	10	601	63*	778	968	909	923*	3013	853	3756	1037	3843	1089*		
352	9	602	57	779	380*	910	230	3021	905*	3760	162*	3844	410*		

ACKNOWLEDGMENTS

It has been a nostalgic journey preparing this book and I would like to thank all the people who have contributed during the past two decades while I have attempted to be an author – to all the contributors, stitchers, suppliers and in many cases, special friends, who have continued to support me on and off the word processor!

Thank you to my long-suffering family who have lived with (and grown up with) an author in the house, particularly my daughter, Louise, who was six weeks old and had three-month colic when I started to write my first book!

To Bill and James, who have continued to offer humorous contributions to my work; my father and mother, Eric and Pat Fowler, who continue to believe in me and Sue Hawkins and Vivienne Wells, without whom the work would not get done! Thanks to Helen Beecroft and Daphne Cording, the team at Cross Stitch Guild HQ, who keep all sorts of things going while I scribble.

Many thanks to my marvellous team of stitchers and pattern testers both past and present: Hanne Fentiman, Dorothy Presley, Barbara Webster, Lesley Clegg, Sue Moir, Jill Vaughan, Glenys Thorne, Margaret Cornish, Margaret Pallant, Susan Bridgens and Suzanne Spencer.

Thanks to all the generous suppliers of the materials and equipment required for this book: Rainer Steimann of Zweigart for lovely fabrics, DMC Creative World and Coats Crafts UK for stranded cottons and Ian Lawson Smith for his wonderful I-L Soft charting software. And to all the other manufacturers who supplied anything I asked for whilst writing this book.

Thanks to Cheryl Brown at David & Charles for continuing to have faith in me and Linda Clements for her tireless work checking yet another manuscript! A special thank you to Ethan Danielson for all the excellent technical stitch diagrams and beautiful charts which make this book so special.

SUPPLIERS

The Cross Stitch Guild

The Cross Stitch Guild was formed in March 1996 and quickly became a worldwide organization with a committed and enthusiastic body of members – over 2,000 in the first six months of operation.

As word spreads it is clear that many cross stitch and counted thread addicts around the world are delighted to have a Guild of their own. The CSG has received an extraordinary level of support from designers, retailers, manufacturers and stitchers. Guild members receive a full-colour magazine bi-monthly, including free counted cross stitch designs and technical advice and information. The CSG also supplies cross stitch kits, stitchers' gifts, counted thread classes and a wide range of needlework supplies, including cross stitch fabrics, linen bands, stitching paper, bell-pull ends, buttons, charms (including bees and butterflies), gold-plated needles and Designer Gold charting software. Taster Membership and Full Membership are available all over the world and there is now a comprehensive website for members and non-members with discounted shopping: www.thecrossstitchguild.com
For information and our catalogue contact:
CSG HQ, Yells Yard,
Cirencester Road, Fairford,
Gloucestershire, GL7 4BS, UK.
tel: freephone from the UK 0800 328 9750; from overseas +44 (0) 1285 713799.

Charles Craft Inc

PO Box 1049, Laurinburg, NC 28352, USA
tel: 910 844 3521
email: email@charlescraft.com
www.charlescraft.com
For cross stitch fabrics and many useful pre-finished items such as towels

Coats Crafts UK

PO Box 22, Lingfield Estate, McMullen Road, Darlington, County Durham, DL1 1YQ, UK
tel: +44 (0) 1325 365457
(for a list of stockists)
fax: +44 (0) 1325 338822
For a wide range of needlework supplies, including Anchor threads. Coats also stock some Charles Craft products

Crafty Ribbons

3 Beechwood, Clump Farm, Tin Pot Lane, Blandford, Dorset DT11 7TD, UK
tel: +44 (0) 1258 455889
www.craftyribbons.com
For decorative ribbons

DMC Creative World Ltd

Pullman Road, Wigston, Leicestershire LE18 2DY, UK
tel: +44 (0) 116 281 1040
fax: +44 (0) 116 281 3592
www.dmc/cw.com
For a full range of needlework supplies, including threads and Zweigart fabrics

Framecraft Miniatures Ltd

Unit 3, Isis House, Lindon Road, Brownhills, West Midlands WS8 7BW, UK
tel/fax: 01543 360842
tel (international) +44 1543 453154
www.framecraft.com
For a wide range of ready-made items for embroidery, including cards, trinket pots and pincushions

Gay Bowles Sales Inc

PO Box 1060, Janesville, WI 53547, USA
tel: 608754 9466
fax: 608 754 0665
email: millhill@inwave.com
www.millhill.com
For Mill Hill beads and a US source for Framecraft products

Riverbank Woodcrafts

Unit 9, Bosun's Way, Fairfield Industrial Park, Bill Quay, Gateshead, Tyne and Wear NE10 0OR, UK
tel: +44 07860 355820
fax: +44 0191 3889673
www.riverbank-woodcrafts.co.uk
For wooden boxes and footstools

Viking Loom

22 High Petergate, York, YO1 7EH, UK
tel: +44 (0) 1904 765599
www.vikingloom.co.uk
For bag and purse tops, boxes and a wide range of needlework supplies

About the Author

Jane is largely self-taught, having discovered cross stitch after giving up a 15-year career in nursing to look after her son, James. A neighbour introduced Jane to counted cross stitch and unaffordable antique samplers, so in 1983 she decided to design and stitch her own. Within six months she was marketing her first commercial kits, having discovered a gap in the market for authentic English designs of local Cotswold buildings. From its early beginnings with only £25 in the bank, The Inglestone Collection has grown into an internationally successful business – a major factor in this success being the financial acumen and sales talents of ex-banker Bill Greenoff who joined the company full time in 1990.

Jane's prolific writing career began in 1987 (coinciding with the birth of daughter Louise), the first book being *Cross Stitch Castles and Cottages*, based on the houses for which Jane was already well known. *The Cross Stitcher's Bible* is now published in ten languages, and Jane is now working on her 16th book. In addition, Jane is in constant demand for personal appearances. She has broadcast on BBC local radio on the subjects of needlecraft and business, and appeared as a guest on the Debbie Thrower Show, BBC national radio. She has made two videos and taught classes in the USA at the National Needlearts Association and the International Needlearts Retailers Guild shows. Jane has also starred in a series of programmes for Sky Television called *Stitch Perfect*.

INDEX